P9-DFY-761

no. 1634

MCP
4-12

B-1-14   33.2⁰

ICEBERG, RIGHT AHEAD!

The TRAGEDY of the TITANIC

Stephanie Sammartino McPherson

TWENTY-FIRST CENTURY BOOKS · MINNEAPOLIS

To the memory of all those who sailed on the *Titanic*

The author wishes to thank Jean Reynolds for her insightful comments and editing and Richard McPherson for reading the manuscript and for his unfailing support.

The cover illustration, also used on page 5, shows an artist's rendering of the Titanic *as it sank on April 15, 1912.*

Text copyright © 2012 by Stephanie Sammartino McPherson

All rights reserved. International copyright secured. No part of this book may be reproduced, stored in a retrieval system, or transmitted in any form or by any means—electronic, mechanical, photocopying, recording, or otherwise—without the prior written permission of Lerner Publishing Group, Inc., except for the inclusion of brief quotations in an acknowledged review.

Twenty-First Century Books
A division of Lerner Publishing Group, Inc.
241 First Avenue North
Minneapolis, MN 55401 U.S.A.

Website address: www.lernerbooks.com

Library of Congress Cataloging-in-Publication Data

McPherson, Stephanie Sammartino.
    Iceberg, right ahead! the tragedy of the Titanic / by Stephanie Sammartino McPherson.
        p.   cm.
    Includes bibliographical references and index.
    ISBN 978–0–7613–6756-7 (lib. bdg. : alk. paper)
    1. Titanic (Steamship)—Juvenile literature. 2. Shipwrecks—North Atlantic Ocean—Juvenile literature. I. Title.
G530.T6M39 2012
910.9163'4—dc22   2011002352

Manufactured in the United States of America
2 – DP – 3/1/12

TABLE of CONTENTS

THE VIEW FROM THE CROW'S NEST *showed that all was quiet on the Titanic as it sped through the frigid but calm waters of the North Atlantic in the spring of 1912.*

"ICEBERG, RIGHT AHEAD!"

Lookout Frederick Fleet *stared into the darkness* from the tiny crow's nest high above the deck. The *Titanic* was making good time, slicing through the calm, cold water of the North Atlantic Ocean. But it could be hazardous to travel so rapidly at night. Fleet and his fellow lookout, Reginald Lee, knew they were passing through ice-infested waters. The ship's safety depended on their vigilance in spotting icebergs. Stars sparkled in the clear air, but the moon was a tiny sliver on the evening of April 14, 1912, and offered no light to aid the men in their observations. Fleet detected a faint haze on the horizon. Usually a pair of binoculars was kept in the crow's nest to help the lookouts see distant objects. But the binoculars had been missing throughout the four days of the journey.

At 11:10 P.M., Fleet noticed a mass that stood out in the darkness of the water. It didn't seem large from his perch, about the size of "two tables shoved together," he reckoned. But it blocked the ship's pathway and grew rapidly bigger as the *Titanic* advanced. A feeling of dread came over Fleet as he reached for the alarm bell. "There is ice ahead," he informed Lee tersely. He rang the bell three times as a sign of approaching danger.

Then Fleet put in an emergency telephone call to the bridge, the area from which the captain charts the course of the ship. "What do you see?' asked a voice matter-of-factly.

"Iceberg, right ahead!"

"Thank you." The phone disconnected.

Fleet had done everything he could. With mounting anxiety, he watched the iceberg loom closer and closer. The two lookouts steeled themselves for impact.

With only seconds to spare, the ship began to change its course. Fleet and Lee watched the mountain of ice slip by off the starboard (right) side of the ship. It seemed as if the *Titanic* might travel on safely. Then a harsh scraping sound, followed by an unusual silence, alerted them that something was wrong after all.

Others heard the noise and felt a slight jolt. "Just a little vibration," one passenger would later recall.

TITANIC CAPTAIN EDWARD J. SMITH *was popular with passengers and crew alike. He had been with the White Star Line for nearly thirty years, his most recent assignment being captain of the* Olympic.

Another remembered a sensation "Like rolling over a thousand marbles." The *Titanic*'s captain, Edward Smith, hurried to the bridge. "What have we struck?" he demanded.

THOMAS ANDREWS *began as an apprentice at shipbuilder Harland and Wolff at the age of sixteen, eventually working his way up to managing director. He was the head of the team that worked on the* Titanic *and was a passenger on her maiden voyage.*

Anticipating his captain's commands, First Officer William McMaster Murdoch had already rung the warning bell and ordered the watertight doors deep in the ship's hull to be closed. All seemed normal on the upper decks of the ship. But what about the levels below? Captain Smith sent his fourth officer, Joseph Boxhall, to investigate.

Hurrying toward the bow (front) of the ship, Boxhall descended as far as the lowest passenger level. Although he did not find any damage, he soon began to gather alarming reports from people who had been below. "The ship is making water," carpenter John Hutchinson told him. Jago Smith, a mail clerk looking for the captain, had equally bad news. "The mail hold is filling rapidly."

Meanwhile, Thomas Andrews, the managing director of the shipyard that built the *Titanic*, had come onto the bridge. He knew more about the ship's structure than anyone else on board. Together, Captain Smith and Andrews set out on their own tour to assess damage. The collision with the iceberg had taken place below the waterline. The pressure had caused metal plates to buckle and rivets holding the plates together to pop.

Five forward compartments at the bottom of the ship were flooding rapidly. Although watertight bulkheads separated the ship's lowest compartments, Andrews knew these walls were not tall enough. The water would rise and spill over them into other areas. Quietly Andrews broke the news to Captain Smith. The *Titanic* was doomed.

"How long have we?" asked the captain.

"An hour and a half," replied Andrews. "Possibly two. Not much longer."

Edward Smith was a seasoned veteran, perhaps the most respected captain of the White Star Line, the shipping company that owned the *Titanic*. Crew and passengers alike appreciated his thirty-two years of experience and his steady, courteous manner. Some frequent travelers even said they would only sail on a ship captained by Smith. Recently Smith had successfully dealt with two accidents on the *Olympic*, the *Titanic*'s sister ship. But he had never faced a catastrophe of the magnitude before him. With grim determination, he began preparations to evacuate the ship.

Roused from sleep or from card games and conversation, many passengers were more confused than alarmed. The huge *Titanic* seemed solid and safe; the water below, dark and forbidding. Pointing to

SMOOTH OCEAN

The calmness of the sea the night of April 14, 1912, may have actually posed a risk to the *Titanic*. If the water had been choppier, waves would have been breaking around the icebergs. This would have made the icebergs easier for the lookouts to spot.

a lifeboat, American millionaire John Jacob Astor told his wife, "We are safer here than in that little boat." Other passengers seemed to agree. The *Titanic* had been built to be the largest, safest ship in the world. It was as long as four city blocks and as tall as an eleven-story building. Newspapers touted the vessel as "unsinkable." The *New York Times* went so far as to call the *Titanic* and other sturdily built ocean liners so "secure against loss by collision, that even after the most violent shock they will be kept afloat."

But as water continued to rise in the *Titanic*, people realized the seriousness of their situation. The ocean liner did not have nearly enough lifeboats for the more than two thousand people on board. Under captain's orders, the crew followed the time-honored practice of "Women and children first." But some women refused to leave their husbands. Others may have believed the ship would stay afloat for many hours. A rescue ship would surely arrive before the *Titanic* sank.

Although some men were allowed to board lifeboats when women did not claim vacant seats, most boats were not filled to capacity when they were lowered into the ocean. The officers were afraid that the davits that supported the lifeboats as they descended to the water would break if all the available places were occupied.

At regular intervals, the crew launched flaring rockets as distress signals to catch the notice of any nearby vessels. The ship's wireless (telegraph machine) operators continuously sent out messages asking for help. Despite these measures of hope, it eventually became apparent that no help would arrive in time.

At 2:05 A.M., less than three hours after the collision, the last lifeboat was lowered. Hundreds of people remained on board the *Titanic*. Passengers in the boats watched in anguish as the ship's bow fell deeper into the ocean while its stern (rear) rose into the air. They heard a terrible crash as the *Titanic*'s furniture, its light fixtures, its decorations, and its kitchen equipment slid toward the bow. Those stranded on the ship struggled to keep their balance on the tilting deck. Many fell into the sea. Others held on until the last possible minute. J. Bruce Ismay, the managing director of the White Star Line, huddled in one of the lifeboats. Almost five years earlier, he had helped develop the idea for a luxury ship that would surpass everything else on the ocean. As the end approached, he was helping to row the boat away. He did not see the Titanic's final moments.

By contrast, seventeen-year-old Jack Thayer, struggling in the water, saw it all. Years later, he recalled watching as "one of the funnels seemed to be

WHAT DAMAGE DID THE *TITANIC* SUSTAIN?

For many years, historians believed that the iceberg with which the *Titanic* collided opened a 300-foot (91-meter) gash in the *Titanic*'s side. Recent evidence, however, questions this conclusion. It appears that the ship's rivets gave way, opening up a number of small holes. Although the damage would not have appeared great at first, intense water pressure forced the seawater through the openings at an incredibly rapid rate.

THIS PHOTOGRAPH WAS TAKEN FROM THE *MINIA*, *which was one of the first ships to reach the* Titanic *following the disaster. The crew of the* Minia *found debris and bodies floating in the area around this iceberg and concluded that this was the one that the* Titanic *struck.*

lifted off and fell towards me about fifteen yards [14 m] away, with a mass of sparks and steam coming out of it. I saw the ship in a sort of red glare, and it seemed to me that she broke in two just in front of the third funnel." The resulting waves swamped Jack, pulling him helplessly under the water. When he surfaced again, his hand struck against an overturned lifeboat. A man on top of the boat pulled Jack aboard. From his precarious perch, Jack watched in fascinated horror as

the *Titanic* finally went down.

"Pull for your lives or you'll be sucked under!" cried a crew member who commanded another lifeboat. Numb with cold and shock, many women forced themselves to ply the oars. Marian Thayer joined the effort, unaware of the fate of her husband or son. Almost all the women had been separated from a husband, a father, a brother, or an adult son. All they could do was row and wait and pray.

AT THE TIME IT WAS LAUNCHED, THE *TITANIC* was the world's largest ship. The Olympic was about the same length, but the Titanic (below) outweighed her sister ship by several thousand tons.

CHAPTER ONE

THE BIGGEST SHIP IN THE WORLD

One hundred years earlier, no one could have imagined a steamship as spectacular, fast, or safe as the *Titanic* was meant to be. The first steamship to cross the Atlantic, the SS *Savannah*, was actually a hybrid, powered both by sails and by a steam engine. Despite praise from the *New-York Mercantile Advertiser*, the public was reluctant to book passage. Sailors, similarly cautious, had misgivings about signing on with a ship nicknamed the "steam coffin." What if the engine broke? Would the steam-driven paddle wheels be safe in a storm? Could sparks from an engine start a fire?

After a good deal of difficulty, the Savannah Steamship Company managed to assemble a crew. On May 22, 1819, the ship set sail from Georgia. Twenty-nine days and four hours later, she docked in Liverpool, England. The ship went on to receive enthusiastic receptions in Sweden, Russia, Norway, and Denmark. But despite the excitement, the venture did not meet with financial success. Eventually the company sold the ship.

Eighteen years passed before the SS *Great Western* launched on July 19, 1837, from Bristol, England. The age of transatlantic steamship travel was about to begin in earnest. But ocean crossings still left a great deal to be desired. When British author Charles Dickens sailed to the United States in 1842, he had a miserable experience. The passenger areas were cramped. The deck was cluttered with crates and chicken coops. Dickens described one room as "a gigantic hearse with windows on the sides." Water seeped in through cracks in the smoking den, often soaking the entire room.

Conditions improved steadily, however, as steamships became faster and more convenient. In 1870 a British shipping company named White Star launched the most comfortable seagoing vessel yet. Sometimes called the "Mother of Modern Liners," the *Oceanic* featured promenade decks for lounging or strolling in the fresh air, spacious rooms, and running water. Following up with other state-of-the-art vessels, White Star gained a reputation for fast, enjoyable journeys. Its *Britannic* and *Germanic* broke records by completing the run from Britain to the United States in slightly over a week.

White Star's growing success prompted competition. Although Britain was the undisputed leader in transatlantic travel, Germany decided to enter the race too. The new German liners offered roomy, pleasant quarters and cut travel time even further. Rising to the challenge, another British shipping company, Cunard, built two massive and well-appointed ships, the *Lusitania* and *Mauretania*. As the date for the *Lusitania*'s maiden voyage across the Atlantic approached, the splendid vessel was the talk of the shipping industry. Sailors and maritime experts expected the ship to best all previous records. Officials at White Star felt the challenge keenly.

AMBITIOUS PLANS

On a summer night in 1907, two men met at a mansion in London, England, to discuss how the White Star Line should respond to its rival's widely hailed new ships. Bruce Ismay, of the White Star Line, knew Lord William James Pirrie well and had visited his home before. The shipbuilding firm in which Pirrie was a partner, Harland and Wolff, assembled all the vessels for the White Star Line. Success for one company generally meant success for the other.

Carefully the men considered their options. They could not hope to compete with Cunard's new liners on speed. To regain the commercial advantage, they would have to build incredibly large and luxurious ships. For comfort and elegance, the three vessels they planned would surpass everything else on the sea.

Immediately Ismay set architects and drafters to work designing the new ships. At 890 feet (271 m), each vessel would be 100 feet (30 m) longer than the *Lusitania* and 50 percent bigger. No one had ever created a moving object as huge as what Ismay and Pirrie had in mind. They announced their ambitious intentions on September 11, 1907. Even the names of the ships, revealed seven months later, emphasized their vast size. The vessels were to be called the *Olympic*, the *Titanic*, and the *Gigantic*.

The *Titanic* and her sister ships were to have nine decks. The topmost deck was designated the weather deck. The next seven would be given letters from *A* to *G*. The bottom deck would be the orlop deck, the lowest deck of a ship with four or more decks. Enormous boilers below the orlop deck would create the steam used to run the ship's engines.

The vessels were to be so immense that the Harland and Wolff shipbuilding yard in Belfast, Northern Ireland, had no construction area large enough to accommodate them. Three berths (areas where ships lie at anchor or at a wharf) had to be reconfigured into

LORD WILLIAM JAMES PIRRIE *(LEFT)* AND J. BRUCE ISMAY *(RIGHT)* *inspect the hull of the* Titanic *as it is being built. Ismay succeeded his father as managing director of the White Star Line. His actions as the highest-ranking White Star official to survive the sinking of the* Titanic *led to a major controversy in the subsequent investigations. Pirrie was a partner at the shipbuilding firm Harland and Wolff, builder of all the White Star Line ships. He was lord mayor of Belfast from 1896 to 1897 and was dubbed Viscount Pirrie when King George V visited Belfast in 1921.*

THE *TITANIC* AND ITS TWO SISTER SHIPS, THE *OLYMPIC (TOP)* AND THE *GIGANTIC (BOTTOM),* LATER RENAMED THE *BRITANNIC, were White Star's answer to the Cunard Line's* Lusitania *and* Mauretania. *White Star officials emphasized ultimate luxury on their three premier ships, knowing they could not compete with Cunard on speed.*

two to fit the scale of the *Olympic* and the *Titanic*. The scaffoldlike framework known as the gantry and used in building the ship's hull was 200 feet (61 m) high. This was taller than any other gantry at the time.

The unparalleled size of the *Olympic* and the *Titanic* posed problems on both sides of the Atlantic. Like the Belfast shipyard, New York Harbor to which the ships would sail had to make modifications. No piers in New York were long enough to dock them. At first the harbor board refused permission to extend the piers. But the city's merchants, believing the giant ships would be good for trade, brought the matter to the attention of the U.S. War Department in Washington, D.C. Their persistence paid off. The White Star Line got the go-ahead to lengthen its piers in New York.

"A SHIP SO MONSTROUS"

Work proceeded rapidly on the building of the first two of the three ships. In December 1908, workers laid down the *Olympic*'s keel, the plank at the bottom of the ship that stretches from bow to stern. About three months later, on March 22, 1909, work began on the *Titanic*. Once the keel was in place, workers began building up the sides. For a long time, the structure bore no resemblance to a ship. Then Belfast observers began to see something almost uncanny.

INTERNATIONAL MERCANTILE MARINE COMPANY

The White Star Line started out as a British company. By the time the *Titanic* was built, the company had been transferred to American ownership. J. P. Morgan, one of the wealthiest men in the United States, bought White Star in 1902. It became part of his International Mercantile Marine Company (IMM), which included a number of other shipping lines. The situation did not sit well with many British citizens. The government was disturbed enough to help the British-owned Cunard Company finance the building of *Lusitania* and *Mauretania*. The British magazine, *Fairplay*, summed up the general consternation in May 1905:

> What most people do feel is the keenest regret that such a magnificent line as the White Star, not to mention the other great lines associated with it, should have passed from British to American ownership, from British to American control.

The fact that White Star ships still flew the British flag was called "nothing less than a public scandal."

"A skeleton within the scaffolding began to take shape," recalled one man, "at the sight of which men held their breaths. It was the shape of a ship, a ship so monstrous and unthinkable that it towered over the buildings and dwarfed the very mountains by the water."

Construction was grueling work, but the men took pride in their accomplishment. A caulker who had been hired to fill in crevices to make the ship watertight expressed great enthusiasm for his job. "Well, I loved it, I loved it, and I loved my work and I loved the men. . . . If you had seen or known the process of extra work that went into the ship, you'd say it was impossible to sink her. . . . Yes, it was a marvelous bit of work."

STATE-OF-THE-ART CONSTRUCTION

The caulker had good reason for his optimism. The *Titanic*'s hull had a double bottom so that if its outer layer was pierced, it would still remain afloat. The space between the two skins was wide enough for a person to stand upright. The hull's interior was also structured to assure safety. The *Titanic*'s designers had taken a lesson from an accident that befell the Guion Line's *Arizona*.

In 1879, its first year in service, the *Arizona* struck an iceberg. The sudden impact greatly damaged the bow of the ship. But the vessel's hull was divided into compartments by a series of watertight bulkheads. When water filled one compartment, the next compartment remained dry. Stern first, the *Arizona* was able to limp safely back to Saint John's, Newfoundland, in Canada. By copying the series of watertight compartments, the *Titanic*'s design team thought they had guaranteed their vessel's safety in a similar collision.

GALA LAUNCHING

The building of the *Titanic* and the *Olympic* dominated the town of Belfast. When the *Titanic* was launched into the water on May 31, 1911, the residents turned out in droves. Spectators from elsewhere included more than one hundred news reporters as well as J. P. Morgan, who had a huge stake in the success of the vessel. Those lucky enough to hold tickets had prime seats in the grandstands. More than one hundred thousand people crammed into the shipyard and lined the riverbank for the gala event. They climbed onto rooftops and hung from the masts of ships, hoping for a glimpse of the ship as it slid into the water.

TO ACCOMMODATE THE CONSTRUCTION OF THE *TITANIC* AND THE *OLYMPIC*, the Harland and Wolff shipyard had to build an elaborate scaffolding system known as the Arrol Gantry, or the Great Gantry. The Arrol Gantry was a part of Belfast's skyline for many years. It remained in use until the 1960s. Yard workers riveted more than two thousand steel plates, each 1 inch (2.5 centimeters) thick, into the ship's framework.

At 12:10 P.M., officials fired a rocket. Several seconds passed before workers standing on the dock noticed any movement. Slowly the ship glided toward the water. Tugboats blew their whistles, spectators cheered as the *Titanic* gained momentum down the carefully greased launching ramp. Sixty-two seconds later, the great ship entered the water. The show was over, and the most important guests headed to the Grand Central Hotel for a celebratory launch lunch.

FITTING OUT

The first stage in the *Titanic*'s construction was over. But the ship was still an empty shell. After her festive launching, the *Titanic* was towed to a deepwater wharf to be fitted with boilers, engines, and electric generators. The addition of four huge funnels, or smokestacks (three connected to the boiler rooms and one a dummy), made the *Titanic* an even more impressive sight.

The public's imagination was most captured by the splendor of the interior. White Star spared no expense to make its ship the equal of the finest hotel on land. Although first-class passengers would enjoy the greatest luxury, those traveling third class were also well provided for. Each traveling class would boast comfortable dining rooms, lounges, and smoking rooms

WORKERS GATHER AT THE SHIPYARD IN BELFAST *to watch the* Titanic *take to the water for the first time on May 31, 1911. The solid bronze side propeller shown in the foreground was one of two. It measures 23 feet 6 inches (7.2 m) across and weighs 38 tons (35 metric tons). The smaller center propeller to its left measured 16 feet 6 inches (5 m) across and was powered by a separate engine.*

as well as spacious promenades and stairways. The first-class grand stairway, with its elegant curves and grand dome, would become one of the most famous features on the ship. First-class passengers not inclined to climb stairs had three elevators at their disposal. Second-class passengers had the use of an elevator as well.

HOW MANY LIFEBOATS?

Alexander Carlisle *(right)*, the first director of the team that designed the *Olympic* and the *Titanic*, wanted another safety feature—forty-eight lifeboats, enough to accommodate 3,120 people. But officials of the White Star Line had other ideas. The *Titanic* was to be the most lavish ship ever built. More lifeboats would take up space that could be used as promenades. The company reduced the number of boats to sixteen wooden lifeboats plus four collapsibles. This met the safety regulations of the British Board of Trade, even though the *Titanic*'s lifeboats would not have enough space for even half the people on board. Officials reasoned that there was no real need for lifeboats. No one could imagine any set of circumstances that would sink the *Titanic*.

After the disaster, a grieving and frustrated Carlisle recalled his initial recommendations: "Personally I consider there were not enough [lifeboats]. . . . I said so over and over again. . . . I said it at the Merchant Shipping Advisory Committee on the 19th and 26th of May [1911] . . . before either of the ships went to sea. I said it to the entire meeting, whoever was present heard me say it. . . . I showed them the plans of my proposals; I could not do any more."

During the ten months in which the *Titanic* was "fitted out," first-class staterooms were decorated in a variety of elegant styles. The two best suites included a sitting room, two bedrooms, two dressing rooms, a private bath, and a private deck. A suite's $4,246 price tag represented a huge sum of money in 1912. But millionaires who made frequent ocean crossings did not flinch at the cost. To further enhance their trip, first-class passengers had access to a swimming pool, a gymnasium, a library, a squash court, Turkish baths (steam rooms) and several fine restaurants. Second-class accommodations, though less grand, included more luxuries than first-class travel on other ships.

ABOVE: THE GREAT PROMENADE *was used by the first-class passengers, but each class had its own promenades and stairwells.*
RIGHT: THE GRAND STAIRCASE *in both the* Titanic *and its sister ship the* Olympic *were identical. It was for the first-class passengers and became one of the most iconic attributes of the* Titanic. *Such luxuries came at a price, however. One hundred years later, the premier first-class one-way fare of $4,375 would be equivalent to approximately $100,000.*

TITANIC IN EVERY SENSE OF THE WORD

The word *titanic* means "colossal" or "immense," and the ship launched in 1911 fit the description from top to bottom. Its funnels were so enormous that a locomotive could fit inside each one. Its three anchors weighed a total of 31 tons (28 metric tons). The *Titanic* had twenty-nine boilers to produce steam. A double-decker tramcar could fit in each one. Its engines were four stories high and generated 55,000 horsepower. As it moved through the ocean, the *Titanic* displaced 45,000 tons (40,823 metric tons) of water.

White Star officials knew they could make money not only from the richest passengers but also from the poorest. Many third-class passengers would be immigrants to the United States. Some would carry all their belongings with them on the ship. Few ever expected to see their homelands again. The *Titanic* provided small but comfortable cabins for families as well as less expensive men's and women's dormitories.

ON ITS WAY

When the *Titanic* was ready to leave Belfast, thousands of people turned out to see it off. The ship made a short run to Southampton, where it was scheduled to begin its maiden voyage on April 10, 1912. Excited passengers, awed by the mammoth vessel, jostled their way down the pier in search of the first-, second-, or third-class gangway. Around noon the gangways were lifted and the cables mooring the ship to the dock released. Lining the decks and peering from windows, passengers called out their last good-byes. Three blasts of the ship's horn signaled immediate departure.

Second-class passenger Charlotte Collyer was not surprised by the crowds on the dock or by the lively scene. The ship itself, however, amazed her. "The *Titanic* was wonderful," she recalled, "far more splendid and huge than I had dreamed of. The other craft in the harbour were like cockle shells [light, flimsy boats] beside her." A friend who accompanied her to the dock wondered if she wasn't scared to risk a voyage across the Atlantic. "What on this boat!" replied Collyer. "Even the worst storm could not harm her!"

LARGE CROWDS TURN OUT TO WATCH THE *TITANIC* leave *Southampton, England, on April 10, 1912. The ship took on passengers as well as nearly seven hundred crew members at this port.*

THE *TITANIC* ALMOST HAD A COLLISION *before it even left the harbor in Southampton. Interestingly, while under Captain Smith's command, the Olympic had collided with a navy cruiser and had damaged a tugboat in New York Harbor.*

CHAPTER TWO

FULL SPEED AHEAD

Amid great fanfare, five tugboats pulled the Titanic away from the dock. Then the ship began to move on its own, displacing vast amounts of water as it gained speed. The resulting waves were so strong that another nearby liner, the *New York*, was jarred loose from her moorings. The stout ropes that held it to the dock shattered with a roar like gunfire. While its six-foot (1.8 m) gangway collapsed into the water, the helpless *New York* was swept into a collision course with the *Titanic*. Taking swift action, Captain Smith and the captain of the tugboat *Vulcan* managed to avert the catastrophe. But passengers and spectators held their breath as the *New York* came within several feet of the great *Titanic*.

Shaken by the close call, some regarded the incident as a warning. "That's a bad omen," said second-class passenger Thomas Brown to his daughter. But most passengers regarded the near accident as little more than a nuisance. "It didn't frighten anyone," said Charlotte Collyer, still enthralled by the ship's enormous size. "It only seemed to prove how powerful the Titanic was."

SMOOTH SAILING

As the ship left for its next port of call—Cherbourg, France—passengers began exploring their surroundings. Even crew members, who had boarded several days before the passengers, had a hard time finding their bearings. Second Officer Charles Lightoller would recall that it took him two weeks before he "could find [his] way with confidence from one part of the ship to another."

In Cherbourg some of the most distinguished people making the voyage came aboard, including John Jacob Astor, the wealthiest man on the ship. Then the *Titanic* sailed to Queenstown, Ireland, where 123 more passengers came aboard. With a total of 1,296 passengers and 918 crew members, the ship set off on her transatlantic journey. The weather was perfect, and passengers were delighted with the steadiness of the ship. Few had to worry about

TITANIC PASSENGER JOHN JACOB ASTOR IV *was believed to be the wealthiest passenger on board the* Titanic, *with a family fortune of approximately $150 million.*

seasickness. As passenger Washington Dodge recalled, "At all times, one might walk the decks with the same security as if walking down Market Street [a main street in San Francisco, California], so little motion was there to the vessel."

The stability made it all the easier for passengers to enjoy the ship's many amenities, which *Titanic* traveler Lawrence Beesley listed enthusiastically.

LAST *TITANIC* PHOTOS

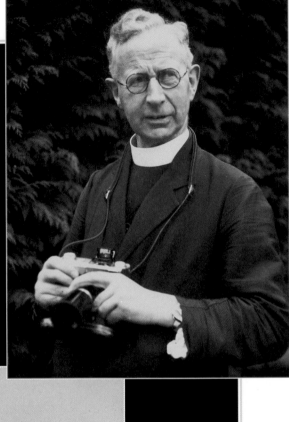

Frank Browne, a student of theology in Dublin, Ireland, received a generous gift from his uncle—a first-class ticket for the first two legs of the *Titanic*'s maiden journey. He enjoyed the trip to Cherbourg, France, and on to Queenstown, Ireland, very much. Greatly interested in photography, he took many photos of the ship. When an American passenger offered to pay his fare all the way to New York, he telegraphed his superior at the Jesuit seminary for permission. The reply came swiftly. "Get off that ship!"

Browne left the ship as ordered, but very shortly newspapers all over the world would use his photographs in their coverage of the *Titanic* disaster. These included the last photo of Captain Smith, the only photo ever made of the wireless room, and a photo of wireless operator Harold Bride *(see photo on page 34)*. After his death in 1960, Father Browne's negatives of the *Titanic* lay forgotten for more than twenty-five years. When they were discovered in 1986, the *London Sunday Times* called them "the photographic equivalent to the discovery of the Dead Sea Scrolls [the oldest known copies of biblical texts and other documents dating from as early as 150 B.C.]."

TOP: FATHER FRANK BROWNE *poses with his camera years after the* Titanic *disaster.*
BOTTOM: THE PHOTOS *Father Browne took on the first part of the journey were some of the last photos of the ship and crew. This is a photo of the dock at Queenstown, Ireland, where Father Browne got off the ship.*

"There is an uninterrupted deck run of 165 yards [151 m] for exercise and a ripping [terrific] swimming bath, gymnasium and squash racket court & huge lounge & surrounding verandahs." No wonder Beesley said that the ship was "like a palace."

Four days into the voyage, Captain Smith decided to make a change in the traditional routine of ocean voyages. Usually Sundays at sea began with a lifeboat drill. Instead, the captain held a religious service for all passengers. Especially good dinners were served in the various dining rooms that day. Then passengers enjoyed a relaxing afternoon on a sea that was, according to Second Officer Lightoller, "like glass."

WARNINGS

Throughout the day, as people lounged and visited with one another, the temperature dropped sharply. The ship's wireless operators, busy sending out telegrams for passengers, began receiving warnings of ice in the ship's vicinity. The first message came from a nearby ship, the SS *Caronia*, warning of "bergs, growlers, and field ice." Almost five hours

ICEBERGS AND GROWLERS

The winter of 1912 had been unusually mild in the polar regions. This created a greater problem than usual in the North Atlantic shipping lanes. The warmer temperatures had caused more icebergs than usual to break off the polar ice shelves. But in more southern waters, the situation was reversed. Colder-than-usual temperatures prevented the icebergs from melting as quickly as in past years. These two factors resulted in the huge ice field in the *Titanic*'s path.

Berg means "mountain" in some northern European languages, and icebergs are indeed immense. A very large iceberg can loom more than 240 feet (75 m) high and stretch more than 670 feet (204 m) wide. Even a small iceberg rises 14 to 50 feet (5 to 15 m). Very small icebergs, classified as bergy bits, are from 3 to 14 feet (1 to 4 m) high. The smallest of all, growlers are less than 3 feet (1 m) high. As huge (or as small) as an iceberg may appear, most of its mass lies below the surface of the water.

later, Captain Smith received a second warning. Choosing to share the information with Ismay, Smith handed him the written message. Ismay tucked the warning into his pocket and went to lunch. During the afternoon, he showed the warning to several passengers.

"I suppose you are going to slow her [the ship] down," commented Emily Ryerson when she learned of the ice field.

Ismay must have startled her. "Oh no," he is said to have replied. "On the contrary, we are going to let her run a great deal faster and get out of it."

Some historians believe the *Titanic* received as many as seven ice warnings throughout the day. That evening Captain Smith reclaimed the message he had given to Ismay and posted it for the officers navigating the ship. He also changed the ship's course to the south, where they would be less likely to encounter ice.

By nightfall the temperature had plunged to freezing. Second Officer Lightoller commented on the cold when he retired for the evening. Aware of some of the ice warnings, he instructed the lookouts, Frederick Fleet and Reginald Lee, to be especially vigilant. Despite the bitter chill, the weather was beautiful. "It was a brilliant, starry night," teenage passenger Jack Thayer would later recall. "There was

BEHIND THE SCENES

The first days of the *Titanic*'s voyage seemed perfect. However, a few glitches occurred without passengers' knowledge. A fire had been simmering in one of the ship's coal bunkers since the departure from Belfast. Although controlled, it wasn't put out for several days. In addition, the ship's wireless broke down on Friday, April 12. The two operators, Harold Bride and John "Jack" George Phillips *(right)*, weren't able to get it going again until early Saturday morning. This meant that many passengers' telegrams had to be delayed. Bride and Phillips still hadn't caught up on the backlog when ice warnings began coming in on Sunday.

no moon, and I have never seen the stars shine brighter; they appeared to stand out of the sky, sparkling like diamonds. . . . It was the kind of night that made one feel glad to be alive."

"WE ARE STOPPED AND SURROUNDED BY ICE"

Ice alerts continued to arrive. At 9:40 P.M., wireless operator Jack Phillips received a message from the *Mesaba*, warning of "heavy pack ice and great number large icebergs, also field ice. . . ." Phillips, who was alone in the wireless room (his colleague was sleeping), couldn't leave his station to take the warning to the bridge. Overworked with sending messages for passengers, he had little patience when the final ice warning came around 11 P.M., from the *Californian*. "Say, old man, we are stopped and surrounded by ice," wired the ship's operator, Cyril Evans.

Evans didn't have a chance to give the *Californian*'s coordinates before Phillips replied brusquely, "Shut up, shut up; I am working Cape Race [he was in the process of connecting with a Newfoundland, Canada station], you are jamming

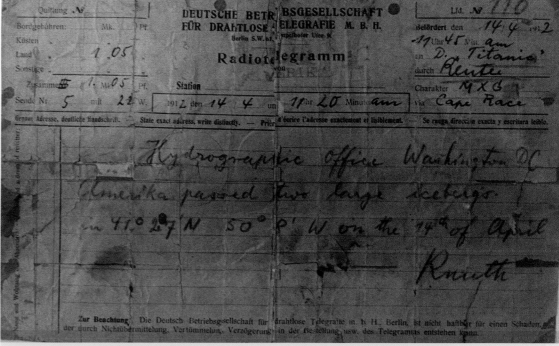

ON APRIL 14, 1912, THIS TELEGRAM *was sent by the Hamburg-American Line steamship* Amerika. *It was one of a number of telegrams from different sources received on board the* Titanic *warning of the presence of ice in the vicinity.*

me." Such curt replies were not unusual, and Evans decided not to press the matter. He turned off the wireless set and went to bed.

Many passengers were also turning in for the night as the *Titanic* continued to race through the water. She was going 22.5 knots (26 miles [42 kilometers] per hour). This was as fast as she had gone on the entire journey.

THE *TITANIC* APPROACHES AN ICEBERG *in this twentieth-century painting by British artist C. J. Ashford. Note that smoke is only coming from the first three smokestacks. The fourth one was a "fake" stack, added for ventilation and to enhance the profile of the ship.*

CHAPTER THREE

MAN THE LIFEBOATS

Second Officer Lightoller was almost asleep when he "felt a sudden vibrating jar rush through the ship." He shot out of bed and hurried to the deck in his pajamas. He leaned over the port (left) side and then dashed around to the starboard side, but he could see nothing in the blackness. The bitter cold pierced him, and he decided to return to his quarters. If he were needed later on (as he guessed he would be), his fellow officers would expect to find him in his room.

Lightoller returned to bed and waited. About ten minutes later, Fourth Officer Boxhall arrived. "We've hit an iceberg."

"I know you've hit something," replied Lightoller.

"The water is up to F deck in the Mail Room."

That was all Lightoller needed to hear. Soon he was properly dressed and back on deck, ready to face the nightmare of his life.

"YOU HAVEN'T A HALF HOUR TO LIVE"

A trimmer who supplied coal for the stokers to put into the furnaces, Samuel Hemming, was also in bed when he felt the impact. He peered through the porthole and listened intently. A strange hissing noise puzzled him. It took him a moment to realize that air was leaking from a tank as ocean water poured in. Not knowing what to do, Hemming returned to bed. Suddenly the ship's boatswain (supervisor of unlicensed deckhands) was at the door. "Turn out you fellows," he cried. "You haven't half an hour to live. This is from Mr. Andrews. Keep it to yourselves and let no one know."

Those on duty even deeper in the ship needed no such dire pronouncement to realize the *Titanic* was in serious trouble. In boiler room 6, Second Engineer James Hesketh was chatting with Frederick Barrett, the head stoker. A red warning light silenced them abruptly. Then a rasping metallic noise, followed by an earsplitting boom, rocked the room. Almost instantly the sea came roaring through a hole about 2 feet (0.6

THE SENIOR CREW OF THE *TITANIC* *photographed on board the ship.* Back row (left to right): *Herbert McElroy, Charles Lightoller, Herbert Pitman, Joseph Boxhall, Harold Lowe.* Front row (left to right): *James Moody, Henry Wilde, Captain Edward Smith, and William Murdoch. These men led a staff and crew of more than 850 people.*

m) above the floor. The two men barely had time to get out before the watertight door, activated from the bridge, slammed shut behind them.

Several stokers from the boiler rooms reached the higher decks only to be sent below again to deal with the extreme pressures that were building up in the boilers. Not only were they in danger from the rising water, but fire and explosions posed real threats also. "We certainly had a Hell of a time putting those fires out," a stoker from boiler room 5 would recall years later.

"MY FIRST GRIP OF FEAR"

Confused and curious passengers were beginning to investigate what the sensation of jerking had meant and why the engines had gone silent. Charlotte Collyer sought information from a stoker whom she saw emerging from the lower levels. Covered with blood and coal dust, the man had lost all the fingers on one hand. "Danger!" roared the man in response to her query. "I should say so! It's hell down below. The boat will sink like a stone in ten minutes." Collyer watched the man stumble away, lie down, and lose consciousness. "At this moment I got my first grip of fear—awful sickening fear. That poor man with his bleeding hand and speckled face brought up a picture of smashed engines and mangled human bodies," she recalled.

CHARLOTTE COLLYER *remembers the fear she felt when she realized the trouble the* Titanic *was in. She is shown here with an unidentified child (probably her daughter Marjorie) and covered with a White Star Line blanket.*

"ONLY A PRECAUTION"

For most first- and second-class passengers, however, the realization of danger came much more slowly, and the ship's crew members did their best to reassure them. A steward told Lawrence Beesley that he didn't know what had caused the engines to stop, adding, "I don't suppose it's much."

Another steward got the story wrong when he told Emily Ryerson, "There's talk of an iceberg, ma'am, and we've stopped so as not to run over it." Ryerson thought about it a moment and then decided the news was not important enough to awaken her husband.

More curious than alarmed, second-class passenger Winnie Troutt found nothing amiss on the boat deck. Then she noticed several crew members uncovering one lifeboat and lowering another. She hurried to tell her friends what she had seen. On her way, she encountered yet another crew member yelling out, "All passengers put on your lifebelts and go up on top deck. Leave everything. It is only a precaution and you can all return to your staterooms."

Some people laughed at the instructions, but not Winnie. "This ship is going to sink," she emotionally informed a young man she knew. Back in her cabin, she became impatient when her friend Nora Keane refused to leave without putting on her corset [tightly laced undergarment]. Winnie snatched the corset from her, insisting there wasn't a minute to waste.

"ALL PASSENGERS ON DECK"

It was time to warn those passengers who had remained in their rooms. As stewards knocked on the doors of first- and second-class staterooms, they tried to make their summons urgent yet reassuring. They didn't want to start a panic, but they had to get everyone into life jackets and to the decks. In the stress of the moment, the passengers threw life vests over evening gowns or coats over pajamas. Some didn't bother to lace their shoes. Others came barefoot or in stocking feet. Author and passenger Helen Churchill Candee compared the scene to "a fancy-dress ball in Dante's Hell [a section of *Divine Comedy*, a fourteenth-century epic poem describing hell

BRAVE MUSICIANS

After the deafening roar from the funnels ceased, several of the ship's musicians *(some pictured below)* assembled in the first-class lounge and began to play. They hoped the ragtime [lively musical style of the early 1900s] songs they chose would ease anxiety and bolster the passengers' spirits. Other musicians joined them, and eventually they moved out to the boat deck. The men succeeded in their mission of soothing people's nerves. The melodies drifted over the water to those in lifeboats. None of the musicians tried to enter the lifeboats themselves. According to tradition, they kept on playing right up to the ship's final moments. Survivors had different recollections of their final number. Most passengers believed it was the hymn "Nearer My God to Thee."
An exception was wireless operator Harold Bride who, in a *New York Times* interview, said that he heard them playing a song called "Autumn." Whatever the last song was, all agreed that the musicians showed great courage and dedication in the face of disaster.

and its inhabitants written by Dante Alighieri]." But few people were unduly alarmed. One woman seemed to sum up the general confidence when she exclaimed, "Why do they need lifeboats? This ship could smash a hundred icebergs and not feel it."

The level of noise on the boat decks was deafening as the funnels discharged vast clouds of steam from the boilers far below. Normally the steam would have been used to run the engines, but the engines had stopped. People had to yell to make themselves heard above the din. The freezing temperatures pierced through the layers of clothing people had hastily donned. The clamor and the bitter cold drove many passengers back into the lounge or the gymnasium.

MYSTERY SHIP

The ship's crew and many passengers thought that deliverance was at hand when two masthead lights from a steamer became visible in the distance. It seemed to be approaching the *Titanic*. Even before the distress rockets were fired, Fourth Officer Boxhall began to signal the ship with a Morse lamp. The lamp allows crews to use Morse code to send signals of light across the water. "Tell [the ship] to come at once," Captain Smith commanded him. "We are sinking." But no reply came from the nearby ship. Nevertheless, the sight of lights from the steamer strengthened the resolve of some women not to enter a lifeboat and to wait for help from the other ship instead. Eventually the so-called mystery ship disappeared into the night, taking with it all hope of a speedy rescue.

"YOU'LL REMEMBER ME"

Generally, steerage (third-class) passengers, lodged lower in the ship, experienced a more forceful jolt than those in first- and second-class cabins. Aware that something was seriously amiss, some third-class passengers began making their way toward the ship's stern even before crew members called them from their rooms. A number of them carried their luggage, sometimes containing all they had in the world. But there was no easy passageway from third class to the boat deck. Because many steerage passengers were immigrants who spoke little or no English, a good deal of confusion ensued as they tried to figure out what had happened. Often they found their way blocked by gates or by locked doors that separated the accommodations of the various classes. In addition, crew members stopped passengers attempting to leave the third-class area. In desperation, some men

"FOOT BY FOOT"

Those who descended to the sea in lifeboats never forgot the sensation. Lawrence Beesley, a second-class passenger admitted to lifeboat number 13, called it "exciting to feel the boat sink by jerks, foot by foot, . . . thrilling to see the black hull of the ship on one side and the sea, seventy feet [21 m] below, on the other." On the same boat, twelve-year-old Ruth Becker, who had become separated from her mother, "could see the water rushing into the ship." As her boat rowed away, she thought the *Titanic* was a "beautiful sight" with its brightly lit portholes. Deep in the ship, engineers worked to keep the electricity functioning until the very last moment. If it weren't for the "tilt downwards toward the bow," Ruth would have thought all was well in the huge, fine-looking ship.

took a precarious route across cargo cranes into second class. From there they were able to reach the boat deck.

Other third-class passengers remained in the well deck, an enclosed area toward the stern. From this vantage point, they could see lifeboats bobbing in the ocean, but they had no access to them. Two Catholic priests from second class came to offer moral support. Some passengers, determined to preserve an environment of normalcy began dancing to the music of a piano in the smoking room. Others played cards and told jokes. It was a way to remain calm while they awaited further instructions.

Minnie Coutts, the mother of two little boys, was not willing to wait. When the order came to don life belts, she found that there were only two in her cabin. A crew member told her that all the life preservers had already been distributed. But Coutts persisted in her quest. Later, the same crew member led Minnie and her sons down a maze of corridors to his own personal quarters. Producing a belt, he helped Coutts slip it on correctly. "There!" he said. "If the boat goes down, you'll remember me."

Wandering the hallways afterward, however, Minnie began to despair that they would never find their way out of the ship. Finally, she came upon another crew member who showed her an alternate route to the boat deck. Shivering, she held her boys close to her as she watched to see what would happen.

SOS

Captain Edward Smith knew that the only hope to save everyone was if a nearby ship came to the rescue. At 12:10 A.M., he told wireless operators Jack Phillips and Harold Bride *(shown in the ship's wireless room in photo at right)* to begin sending distress calls with the *Titanic*'s approximate latitude and longitude (exact positioning on a map). Immediately Phillips began tapping out *CQD* in Morse code (a telegraph system of dots and dashes to communicate quickly). This was a standard call for assistance. *CQ* alerted the wireless operator at the other end that this message was to take precedence over all others. The *D* stood for danger. Later, Bride suggested, "Send SOS; it's the new call, and it may be your last chance to send it." Both men still believed that the *Titanic* would be saved, and Phillips laughed at what seemed a joke. But he did begin using the SOS signal.

Adopted by the second International Radiotelegraphic Convention, held in Berlin, Germany, in 1906, the SOS signal had been chosen for its simplicity in Morse code—three dots, three dashes, and three dots. It was easy to remember and quick to send. Most wireless operators, however, continued to rely on the CQD call. Phillips and Bride were among the very first, if not the first, to use SOS. After the *Titanic* disaster, the new signal became widely accepted as a sign of distress.

Most of the replies to Phillips's and Bride's distress calls came from ships too distant to arrive before the *Titanic* would sink. The *Olympic*, *Titanic*'s sister ship, was more than 500 miles (805 km) away. The *Carpathia*, only 58 miles (93 km) away, signaled that she would come as swiftly as possible. But Captain Smith knew that even going full speed, the *Carpathia* would take at least four hours to arrive. He also knew that the *Titanic* did not have four hours.

"WOMEN AND CHILDREN FIRST"

A full hour after *Titanic*'s collision with the iceberg, First Officer Murdoch had a difficult time persuading people to enter the lifeboats. Most passengers hesitated to trade the seeming security of the ship for the dark descent to the ocean. "Women and children first!" called out Captain Smith. Second Officer Lightoller echoed the cry, "Women and children first!" But many women refused to leave their husbands.

Ida Straus had one foot on a lifeboat, the other on deck when she turned back to her husband, Isidor, a founder of Macy's Department Store. "We have been living together for many years, and where you go, I go," she declared. When friends urged her to enter the boat, she remained firm. "I will not be separated from my husband. As we have lived, so will we die together."

Someone suggested that Isidor be allowed to enter the boat because of his age. But he proved as resolute as his wife. "I will not go before other men."

"GET IN! GET IN!"

The boat deck had begun to slant noticeably, and the situation was growing desperate.

"Ladies, you *must* get in at once," Thomas Andrews

ISIDOR AND IDA STRAUS *refused to get into lifeboats aboard the* Titanic. *Isidor wouldn't get in before other men, and Ida wouldn't leave her husband behind. The Americans were returning from a European vacation.*

urged. "There is not a moment to lose. You cannot pick and choose your boat. Get in, get in!"

Margaret Brown, a wealthy woman from Denver, Colorado, had just convinced several reluctant women to enter a lifeboat and was looking to see what else she could do to help. Suddenly a crew member came up

LEGENDARY HEROINE

Wealthy first-class passenger Margaret Brown was known for her dynamic personality. As a young mother in Leadville, Colorado, she had joined the National Woman Suffrage Association to fight for women's right to vote. She took a keen interest in educational issues and human rights. After moving to Denver with her family in 1894, she became a charter member of the Denver Women's Club, working to improve women's lives through education. She lost a run for the U.S. Senate in 1909 but kept right on fighting for her social issues. She also worked with a Colorado judge to help poverty-stricken children and to establish the first juvenile court in the United States.

Brown kept the women in her lifeboat rowing even after their boat hooked up with number 16 and Quartermaster Robert Hitchens ordered them to stop. Rowing was a way to keep warm, and she threatened to throw Hitchens overboard if he got in her way. She also shared pieces of clothing with her shivering fellow passengers. She wrapped her expensive sable stole around the legs of a stoker who was shaking from the cold. Throughout the freezing night, she continued to boost morale in the lifeboat.

behind and grasped her tightly. "You are going too!" he declared. Before Margaret knew what was happening, the crew member hoisted her into the air and dropped her 4 feet (1.2 m) into boat number 6.

Other women and children shared a similar experience. Chief Baker Charles Joughin and his crewmates did not bother to ask some women whether they wanted places in a lifeboat. They simply dragged them up to the boat deck and placed them into boat number 10. They also grabbed children and threw them across the gap between the deck and the boat as it hung over the side of the ship.

By contrast, Minnie Coutts faced an overly scrupulous officer who tried to prevent her son William from boarding boat number 2. It seems that the straw hat William wore made him look older than his nine years. But Minnie hadn't made her way from the bowels of the ship only to leave her son behind. She pleaded and protested until the officer finally waved William along to board the boat.

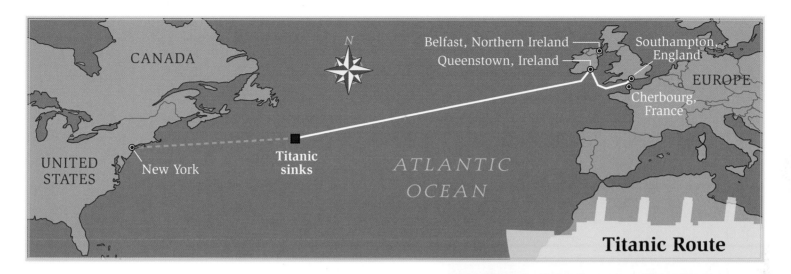

Titanic Route

THE LAST WOODEN BOAT

By the time the last wooden lifeboat, number 4, was ready to launch, fear had long since replaced the earlier confidence in the ship. As number 4 was lowered, two desperate crew members managed to climb onto another boat's empty davits and descend the rigging. This was a risky maneuver for anyone, but the men's bulky life jackets made their movements all the more difficult. One man made it into the boat. The other slipped and fell into the water, but the women in number 4 quickly pulled him aboard.

All that was left were four collapsible lifeboats designated A through D. The *Titanic* was tilting sharply, its bow a mere 10 feet (3 m) above the water. Those still aboard faced a terrifying prospect. They realized that no rescue ship would come before the *Titanic* sank and that their chances of escaping on one of the remaining boats were slim.

FACING THE END IN STYLE

When wealthy American businessman Benjamin Guggenheim realized that the *Titanic* would sink, he decided to go down in style. Assistant Steward James Etches was surprised when he noticed that Guggenheim and his valet, Victor Giglio, had changed into evening clothes. "We are dressed up in our best," explained Guggenheim, "and are prepared to go down like gentlemen. . . . If anything should happen to me, tell my wife in New York that I've done my best in doing my duty."

AN ILLUSTRATION SHOWS *TITANIC* PASSENGERS *waiting to board lifeboats. Note the fear of the young woman in the foreground and the shame of the man holding the suitcase at right. Hands wave from the crowd as couples say their last good-byes. This illustration by Italian artist Fortunino Matania was published in the British magazine Sphere on May 4, 1912.*

CHAPTER FOUR

"SHE'S GONE"

Single and traveling alone, twenty-seven-year-old Winnie Troutt watched the growing turmoil. She saw several men try to force their way onto one of the collapsible boats. On the port side of the ship, First Officer Murdoch did allow men to board when no women came forward. But on the starboard side, Second Officer Lightoller kept to the strict letter of the law. Only women and children were allowed into the lifeboats. Period. Lightoller took a revolver from his pocket and waved it at the men. Unaware that the gun wasn't loaded, the men withdrew. Then crew members joined ranks to form a passage to the boat from which all men were excluded.

Winnie hated to see such painful scenes. She could have joined the women approaching the collapsible boat, but she decided not to. So many families were being torn apart. Winnie decided to stay on the *Titanic* so someone else could have her place.

Abruptly a man cradling a baby appeared before her. "I don't want to be saved," he exclaimed, "but who'll save this baby?"

Immediately Winnie opened her arms to receive the child. With sudden purpose, she walked toward collapsible boat D.

"EVERY MAN FOR HIMSELF"

Throughout the crisis, Harold Bride and Jack Phillips remained at their post, still tapping out distress signals. Suddenly Captain Smith appeared at the door. "Men, you have done your duty," he declared. "You can do no more. Abandon your cabin." When neither man moved, the captain continued, "I release you. That's the way of it now. Every man for himself."

Eventually the two wireless operators climbed to the top of the officers' quarters. They joined the struggle to free the last two collapsibles—lifeboats A and B—that were tied to the roof. Falling off a hastily constructed ramp, boat B landed upside down on the deck. Suddenly, a huge wave flowed over the deck and washed away both boats. Harold Bride, who managed to grab an oarlock, was swept away along with a dozen other people. He found himself trapped beneath the overturned boat B.

As the bow of the *Titanic* sank rapidly, frantic passengers began to climb the increasingly tilting deck to the stern. A sudden influx of steerage passengers from below blocked their way, adding to the confusion and panic. Passenger Archibald Gracie was shocked to note so many women among the steerage passengers. He had thought that most women had made it into lifeboats.

THE *TITANIC* HAD SIXTEEN WOODEN LIFEBOATS *and four collapsible lifeboats like this one on board. The collapsibles were designed to take forty-seven people.*

The end was so near that some passengers and crew members dove into the ocean. Young Jack Thayer, also in the water, watched at a distance of 40 yards (37 m). "The ship seemed to be surrounded with a glare, and stood out of the night as though she were on fire," he recalled. "I don't know why I didn't keep swimming away. Fascinated, I seemed tied to the spot."

Second Officer Lightoller, still on the roof of the officers' quarters, made the same split-second decision as some of his crewmates. Rather than prolong the inevitable, he too dove into the ocean. The freezing water felt "like a thousand knives being driven into one's body," he later recalled. For several agonizing moments, the water pinned Lightoller against the huge metal grating of an air shaft. Freed by a sudden rush of air from the ventilator, he managed to reach boat B and grabbed a rope dangling from its side.

"I CANNOT LOOK ANYMORE"

As the ship slanted more sharply, the rumble of falling objects grew to a deafening roar as deck chairs, luggage, boilers, kitchenware, athletic equipment, and engines came rushing down the slope. One of the ship's great funnels crashed into the passengers floundering in the water. It just missed boat B and Second Officer Lightoller. The resulting wave washed many people off the top of the overturned lifeboat.

According to traditionally accepted accounts, the *Titanic*'s stern thrust up until it was almost perpendicular with the water. More passengers jumped or simply slid off the boat into the water. Others, like baker Charles Joughin, held on until the last possible moment. "I cannot look any longer," said one lifeboat passenger just before the sea closed over the ship. Those who watched helplessly never forgot the sight. "She's gone," whispered the men on boat B almost reverently.

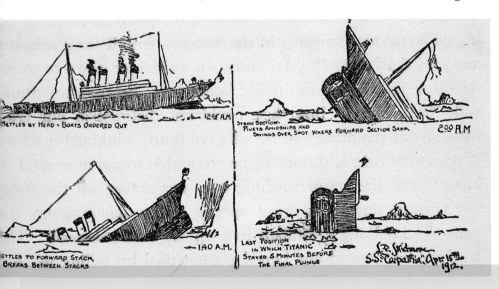

PASSENGER JACK THAYER, *only seventeen when he was on board the* Titanic, *later drew these sketches of what the* Titanic *looked like as it sank.*

"SAVE ONE LIFE"

Hundreds of people struggled in the ocean, buoyed by life jackets but crying out for help as the cold numbed their bodies. Most of the lifeboats had rowed away from the area where the ship sank. But the last two collapsibles were within reach of many who were thrashing in the water. More than two dozen people made it to boat A, half submerging the fragile craft. Even more people scrambled onto the inverted boat B. These included Second Officer Lightoller, Jack Thayer, and Harold Bride, who had finally managed to emerge from underneath the lifeboat.

"Save one life! Save one life!" The cry rang out frequently as someone floundering in the water begged for assistance. With thirty men aboard, collapsible boat B was already loaded to capacity. Steward Thomas Whiteley and stoker Harry Senior tried to climb aboard, only to confront someone blocking their progress with an oar. Fiercely, the men persisted and pulled themselves onto the boat.

Another nearby swimmer was not so insistent. "Hold on to what you have, old boy!" a crew member cried out to him. "One more of you aboard would sink us all."

"That's all right, boys; keep cool," replied the swimmer in a surprisingly hearty voice. "Good luck and

THIS PAINTING OF THE LAST MOMENTS OF THE *TITANIC* is haunting and beautiful, although it is doubtful that the sky was showing the pink of sunrise as the ship was sinking. The ship disappeared at 2:20 A.M., and eyewitnesses reported the sky turning pink just as the Carpathia arrived, which would have been about 4:10 A.M.

God bless you." And he paddled away. Several men later maintained that Captain Smith was the swimmer.

In the midst of their ordeal, the survivors on boat B joined together in saying the Lord's Prayer. The people in boat A also prayed. They were standing up to their knees in water, as the boat settled deeper into the ocean.

"REMEMBER
I WANTED TO GO BACK"

Most of the wooden lifeboats had empty places, but few people aboard were willing to risk their own safety by rowing back to those in the water. Like some of those in the collapsibles, they feared that the frenzy of too many people trying to climb aboard would overturn their boats. Although several people in boat number 8 urged a return to the scene, the other passengers outvoted them. Sailor Thomas Jones was deeply distressed. "If any of us are saved," he declared, "remember I wanted to go back. I would rather drown with them than leave them."

Fifth Officer Harold Lowe refused to let anyone stop him from a rescue mission. He managed to gather four other boats to his own number 14 and tie them together. Then he assigned his fifty-five passengers to places in other boats and chose volunteers to help him row back to the site of the disaster. With a boat almost empty, he had plenty of room for survivors. But all his preparations had taken time. It was after 3 A.M. when boat 14 reached the area where the ship had gone down. People had been gasping and shaking in the 28°F (−2°C) water for almost an hour. Although he occasionally heard

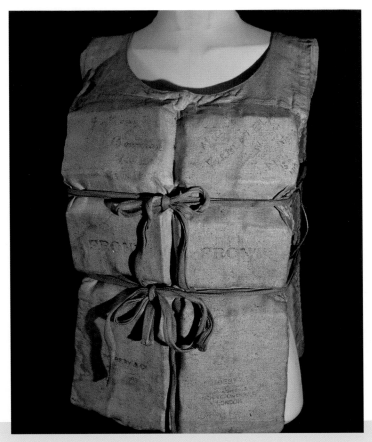

THIS LIFE JACKET FROM THE *TITANIC* *was worn by survivor Laura Mabel Francatelli. Even with a life jacket, passengers couldn't survive long in the frigid ocean water. More than three hundred bodies were pulled from the ocean the morning after the Titanic sank, all wearing life jackets.*

shouts in the darkness, Lowe was only able to save four people. One of the four died soon after his rescue.

AN ILLUSTRATION SHOWS A MAN REACHING OUT TO
PEOPLE IN A LIFEBOAT *as the* Titanic *sinks in the background. The*
buttons on his sleeve indicate that he might be one of the ship's officers.

ADRIFT IN THE SEA

During the long cold night, the survivors discussed
the likelihood that another ship would arrive in
time to rescue them. "The sea will be covered with
ships tomorrow morning," someone predicted. But
others were less optimistic. "We may knock about
here days before we are picked up at all," lamented

GOOD DEED OR BRIBE?

In the weeks after the disaster, a small controversy grew
around boat number 2. Many people found it disgraceful
that the vessel, with only twelve people, did not return to
the wreckage site to aid those in the water. An incident
on board added to the sense of scandal. A discussion
between Sir Cosmo Duff-Gordon (a Scottish landowner and
sportsman) and stoker Robert William Pusey highlighted the
great difference between their social positions and personal
resources. Although Duff-Gordon and his wife lost all the
possessions they had taken on the trip, they could easily
afford to replace them. Speaking for the crew members on
the boat, Pusey declared, "Well, we have lost our [sailor's]
kit [bag containing personal items such as clothes, towels,
and bedding] and the company won't give us any more.
And what's more, our pay stops from tonight."

"Very well," replied Duff-Gordon, "I will give you
a fiver [five English pounds] each to start a new kit."
Duff-Gordon kept his word, but the general public would
look upon his offer with skepticism. It seemed as if Duff-
Gordon was bribing the crew not to return to the scene.
Although he was cleared from any wrongdoing at the
later British investigation into the tragedy, he was never
able to live down the disgrace. He spent the rest of his
life in seclusion.

a crew member. Only those aboard collapsible boat B had accurate news. Wireless operator Harold Bride could tell them that the *Baltic*, the *Olympic*, and the *Carpathia* had replied to the *Titanic*'s distress calls. The heartening news, however, could not lessen the plight of boat B, barely afloat and in constant danger of being swamped. Second Officer Lightoller told the men to stand up. He organized them into two columns. As the boat rocked with the swells, he ordered the men to "Lean to the right" or "Lean to the left" to keep the collapsible balanced. But the exhausted men could not keep this up indefinitely. Finally, Lightoller ordered them to rest. Waves splashed over their feet. Salt spray hit them in the face and stung their eyes. Two men, unable to fight fatigue any longer, slid off the boat and were swallowed by the sea. Those still on board could only hope that help would arrive in time.

MIRACULOUS SURVIVAL

During the crisis, thirty-two-year-old chief baker Charles Joughin put others first and did his job to the best of his ability. He remembered the need for provisions when the order came to man the lifeboats. According to one estimate, he and his assistants supplied 500 pounds (227 kilograms) of bread to the boats before they were launched. When the *Titanic* was close to going under, he threw about fifty deck chairs into the water. He thought that swimmers clinging to them would be able to keep afloat more easily. Staying on the ship until the last possible moment, Joughin eventually found himself in the water and made it to boat B under Second Officer Lightoller's command. Although there was no room on the overcrowded boat, a friend recognized Joughin and reached out to him. Submerged in the water, Joughin held onto his hand throughout the night.

Most of those in the water succumbed to hypothermia (lowering of body temperature) before help could arrive. Some have attributed Joughin's survival to the amount of whiskey he drank during the crisis. The liquor may have helped warm him. Whatever the cause, his was considered an almost miraculous survival.

TITANIC DEMOGRAPHICS

Statistics on the number of people on the *Titanic*'s maiden voyage vary from about 2,207 to 2,228. According to the well-documented website by John R. Henderson of Ithaca College Library of Ithaca, New York, the best estimate of the total number of people on board was 2,214.

- 319 first-class passengers
- 269 second-class passengers
- 699 third-class passengers
- 918 crew members, staff, and personal servants

The exact number of survivors is also in question. Estimates range from 701 to 713. The number 705 is frequently cited.

- 200 first-class passengers survived.
- 117 second-class passengers survived.
- 172 third-class passengers survived.
- 216 crew members, staff, and personal servants survived.

First-class passengers had the best survival rates. The statistics for first and second class do not include servants.

97 percent of the 141 women in first class survived.
86 percent of the 7 children in first class survived. (One child died).
34 percent of the 171 men in first class survived.

86 percent of the 92 women in second class survived.
All the 25 children in second class survived.
8 percent of the 152 men in second class survived.

49 percent of the 179 women in third class survived.
31 percent of the 80 children in third class survived.
13 percent of the 440 men in third class survived.

Overall, 63 percent of the first-class passengers and 43 percent of the second-class passengers survived. Only 25 percent of the third-class passengers survived.

Of the 306 American passengers on board, 58 percent survived.

Of the 327 British passengers on board, 32 percent survived.

THE STEAMER SHIP *CARPATHIA* rushed toward the Titanic at maximum speed under the direction of Captain Arthur Rostron.

CHAPTER FIVE

CARPATHIA TO THE RESCUE

As the Titanic *passengers dealt with fear,* grief, and freezing temperatures, the *Carpathia* was speeding through the ocean, dodging icebergs to reach them. Captain Arthur Rostron had leaped from his bed when his wireless operator and first officer informed him of the *Titanic*'s distress call. He gave orders to reply that the *Carpathia* was coming as swiftly as possible. But the *Titanic* was 58 miles (93 km) away. At *Carpathia*'s top speed of 14.5 knots, or 17 miles (27 km) per hour, Rostron feared they would not arrive in time. He instructed his chief engineer to conserve as much steam as possible and channel it into the boilers. The additional steam would push the engines to go faster, perhaps up to 17 knots, or 20 miles (31 km) per hour. Although the *Carpathia* would still take three and a half hours to reach the *Titanic*, it was the best Rostron could do.

"COME AS QUICKLY AS POSSIBLE"

Methodically the captain began to prepare for what could be several thousand additional people boarding his ship. He knew the survivors would be freezing and weak. Many would be sick or injured—and traumatized. After updating the ship's doctors, he stationed them in the dining rooms to treat the *Titanic*'s passengers as they arrived. He also ordered the chief steward to prepare coffee, soup, and drinks and to collect blankets. Before the *Titanic* survivors could be cared for, they had to be lifted onto the *Carpathia* from the lifeboats. Rostron instructed his crew to assemble a collection of ladders for those who could climb and sling chairs for those who needed to be lifted on board.

Forty miles (64 km) still separated the *Carpathia* from the scene of the disaster when another message came through. "Come as quickly as possible, old man; the engine room is filling up to the boilers." It was the last message from the *Titanic* that the *Carpathia* would receive.

Rostron kept going at full speed, even after the ship entered an enormous field of ice. Extra lookouts

ARTHUR ROSTRON *captained the* Carpathia *and ordered his ship to get to the* Titanic *as fast as possible. He is shown here in 1926. It is ironic that the hero of the* Titanic *story turned out to be a captain from Cunard, the line with which White Star was competing.*

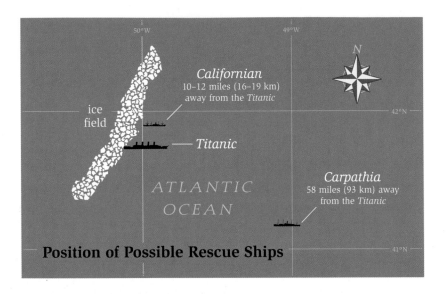

Californian
10–12 miles (16–19 km)
away from the *Titanic*

ice
field

— *Titanic*

Carpathia
58 miles (93 km) away
from the *Titanic*

ATLANTIC
OCEAN

Position of Possible Rescue Ships

APPROACHING LIGHTS

To the *Titanic*'s survivors, the minutes must have seemed like hours. How long could they last in the freezing temperatures? Fourth Officer Boxhall in boat 2 had been sending up flares to alert approaching ships. But only those on board collapsible boat B knew for certain that a ship was speeding to the rescue.

Then a faraway glow became visible in the southeast. A noise like a distant cannon echoed through the air. Finally, the lights of an approaching steamer became apparent. Rockets burst in the sky to signal its coming. Boxhall sent up one last flare to alert the ship of his position. In the greenish light, the *Carpathia*'s crew was able to make out the lifeboat about 300 yards (274 m) away. Rostron began moving the ship into position to pick up the survivors when an enormous iceberg loomed ahead. Veering around it, he approached the boat sideways. "We have only one seaman and can't work very well," called a voice from the boat below.

"All right," yelled Rostron as he maneuvered the ship closer. When the lifeboat was secured fast, a ladder was dropped down. Elizabeth Allen became the first survivor to climb the swaying ladder onto the deck of the *Carpathia*. When everyone in the small boat had boarded, Boxhall was taken to the bridge.

kept watch as starlight glinted from icebergs in all directions. "It was an anxious time with the *Titanic*'s fateful experience very close in our minds," Rostron later recalled. "There were seven-hundred souls on *Carpathia*; these lives, as well as all the survivors of *Titanic* herself, depended on a sudden turn of the wheel."

In the distance, green flares occasionally lit the horizon. Rostron hoped that meant they were nearing the *Titanic*. The *Carpathia* had begun firing rockets too to alert the *Titanic*'s passengers that help was close at hand. But as the *Carpathia* approached the *Titanic*'s coordinates, hope gave way to heightened anxiety. The imperiled ship was nowhere in sight.

THE MOST DRASTIC NIGHT
OF A CAPTAIN'S CAREER

Many years after the rescue, Rostron noted that if the distress call from the *Titanic* had been sent two minutes later, the *Carpathia* would not have received it. Harold Cottam *(shown in telegraphy school in photo at right)*, the *Carpathia*'s wireless operator, had been at his post for many hours. At 12:30 A.M., he finally decided to go to bed. But before he removed his earphones, he bent down to untie his shoes. Suddenly, the wires came alive again. "SOS *Titanic* calling. We have struck ice and require immediate assistance—" According to Rostron, if the *Carpathia* had been 25 miles (40 km) closer, it would have arrived at the *Titanic* in time to save most, if not all, of the passengers and crew members. He would look back on the race to reach the survivors as "the most drastic and memorable night of my career."

Although the *Titanic* was clearly gone, Rostron felt he had to have an official answer. He asked if the ship had sunk.

"She went down at about 2:30," said Boxhall gravely.

"Were many people left on board when she sank?"

"Hundreds and hundreds!" came the anguished reply. "Perhaps a thousand! Perhaps more! My God sir, they've gone down with her. They couldn't live in this icy cold water."

"PULL FOR THE SHORE, BOYS"

The rescue mission had begun. Cheers and exclamations rang out across the water as rowers steered the lifeboats toward the *Carpathia*. Some broke into the song "Pull for the Shore, Boys." Other passengers remained silent, overcome by the tragedy and perhaps cowed by the treacherous beauty around them. Towering icebergs sparkled pink, blue, lavender, and white in the growing light.

The welcome sight of the steamer did not bring the same relief to the men clinging to collapsible boat B.

A SIGHT TO REMEMBER

American impressionist painter Colin Campbell Cooper happened to be aboard the *Carpathia* when the *Titanic* passengers and crew members were rescued from the sea. He and his wife gave up their cabin to the exhausted, emotionally numb survivors. But Cooper wanted to do something more. The beauty and tragedy of the rescue scene haunted him. After the *Carpathia* had delivered the survivors to New York and resumed its passage to the Mediterranean Sea, Cooper completed two paintings. One shows the *Carpathia* cruising past icebergs against an early morning sky. The other shows five small lifeboats approaching the ship, perfectly poised in the middle of the picture between choppy blue water and a pale pink sky. A small iceberg looms to the right.

FAR LEFT: A ROPE LADDER is shown leading from the Carpathia to the lifeboat pulled alongside in this photo taken from on board the rescue ship.
LEFT: SURVIVORS FROM THE *TITANIC* mill around the Carpathia *after being rescued. People eagerly searched for family members whom they hadn't seen since the ship went down.*
ABOVE: SURVIVORS HUDDLE UNDER BLANKETS AND COATS on the deck of the Carpathia *on their way to New York City.*

Four miles (6.4 km) from the *Carpathia*, they feared they could not remain afloat long enough to be rescued. "Ship ahoy!" they yelled frantically, but no one heard. Finally, Second Officer Lightoller blew his whistle, and the piercing sound carried across to a string of four boats tied together. Immediately boats 4 and 12 detached themselves and set off to help. Collapsible B sat so precariously in the water that the waves from number 4 almost washed everyone off. The collapsible continued to lurch as, one by one, the men bridged the gap to one of the wooden boats. As Jack Thayer made his careful way into boat 12, he didn't see his mother seated nearby in number 4. Overwhelmed by her plight, Marian Thayer didn't spot her son either. It wasn't until both were safely aboard the *Carpathia* that their happy reunion took place. But their joy was mixed with sorrow. Jack's father could not be found.

ON TO NEW YORK

After the passengers' initial relief, silence prevailed as the rescue operation continued. Few people expressed either gratitude or their sorrow. Rostron was struck by the stillness. It took four hours for all the people in the lifeboats to climb or be

TRAGIC MISSED OPPORTUNITY

The liner *Californian* was much closer to the *Titanic* than the *Carpathia*. But Captain Stanley Lord knew nothing of the emergency until the next morning after the *Titanic* had already gone down. On encountering an enormous ice field, Stanley had stopped for the night. Around 11:15 P.M., First Officer Charles Groves noted a large brightly lit liner 10 to 12 miles (16 to 19 km) to the east. Less than half an hour later, the liner seemed to stop and then go briefly dark.

The ship did not reply to Morse lamp signals from the *Californian*. Unconcerned, Lord asked to be informed if the ship changed its bearings. It wasn't until about 12:15 A.M. that the *Titanic* sent out its first wireless distress call. By then, Cyril Evans, the *Californian*'s wireless operator, had turned off his set. During the night, several crew members saw white rockets bursting in the sky. Peering through binoculars, Apprentice Officer James Gibson observed that the ship seemed to be slanting in the water. Then the ship appeared to move out of sight. More rockets exploded in the sky around 3:30 A.M. Finally, Chief Officer George Stewart asked Evans to see what he could find out. Turning on the wireless set, Evans learned of the *Titanic*'s crisis. Immediately, Lord headed for the distressed ship but didn't arrive until the survivors were already aboard the *Carpathia*.

hauled onto the *Carpathia*. The very last to arrive was the brave and resourceful Second Officer Lightoller. Long after he clambered aboard, people remained lined along the ship's rail, praying to spy a loved one in the water. Rostron cruised the area too, looking for more survivors. He continued the search while two religious services were held. One was a thanksgiving service for those who had been saved. The other was a memorial for the people who had died.

By 8:50 A.M., another liner, the *Californian*, under Captain Stanley Lord, had arrived. This ship combed the waters in the hope of finding more suvivors while the *Carpathia* headed to New York. Rostron had done all he could to save the *Titanic*'s passengers and crew.

TITANIC BARY

Without her infant son, eighteen-year-old Leah Aks took no interest in her surroundings aboard the *Carpathia*. Her ten-month-old son Philip (called Filly) had been seized from her arms as the *Titanic* sank. A man shouting words she could not understand threw the child overboard. In her horror, Leah was never certain what happened afterward, but eventually she found herself in a lifeboat. Not finding her son on the *Carpathia*, she lay curled on a mattress for two days, in shock. Finally, Selena Cook, who had been next to her in lifeboat 14, forced her to go to the deck for some fresh air. As Leah sat weeping, she thought she heard Filly crying. Suddenly she became aware of an Italian woman holding a baby. To Leah's astonished joy, the baby was Filly! But the other woman, refusing to surrender the baby, rushed off. The child had fallen into her arms as she sat in lifeboat 11. She considered him a gift from God. Selena Cook helped Aks get to the truth. When the two women came together again, Aks described a strawberry birthmark on her son. Then she undressed him and pointed to the mark just as she had described it. Realizing that Aks must be truly the child's mother, the other woman (who was herself pregnant) relinquished the baby. In the press, Filly became known as the "*Titanic* baby."

In 1953 Leah and Philip Aks were guests at a *Titanic* reunion to celebrate Twentieth Century Fox's new movie *Titanic*. When she spotted Selena Cook, Leah Aks raced across the room. "Phil, come meet Selena Cook," she cried. "Without her you may have been lost forever."

CROWDS OF PEOPLE WAIT FOR ANY NEWS OF THE *TITANIC* outside the White Star offices in New York City.

CHAPTER SIX

ARRIVAL IN NEW YORK

The Titanic *had not yet sunk* when Philip Franklin, the White Star Line's vice president in New York, received an early morning phone call. A reporter informed him that the ship had been sending out distress calls and was going down. Though deeply shaken, Franklin had to maintain a strong image for the company. He clung to the hope that everyone on board would be saved.

MISPLACED OPTIMISM

In the absence of hard evidence, newspaper editors tended to adopt the most hopeful view of what had occurred. Faith in the ship's construction led them to believe that the world's greatest ship could not possibly be lost. Mentioning that serious damage was sustained by the *Titanic*, the *Wall Street Journal* also stressed, "She did not sink." Similarly, the *London Daily Mirror* declared "Everyone Safe: Helpless Giant Being Towed to Port."

A mistaken interpretation of several wireless messages added to the misplaced optimism. By noon the *Associated Press* in Montreal, Canada, was ready to issue a bulletin: "All *Titanic* Passengers Safe. The *Virginian* Towing the Liner into Halifax [a coastal city in eastern Canada]." Greatly relieved, Franklin ordered a steamer to meet the two ships and escort them into port. He chartered a train to bring the passengers from Halifax to New York. "We place absolute confidence in the *Titanic*," he told the public. "We believe the boat is unsinkable."

THE *NEW YORK TIMES* GETS IT RIGHT

Readers of the *New York Times* got a different version of the event. Like Franklin, managing editor Carr Van Anda had been shocked at 1:20 A.M. when the newsroom heard that the *Titanic* had struck an iceberg. In researching the event, Van Anda realized that a great deal of time had elapsed since the *Titanic*'s last wireless message. This seemed an ominous sign to him. If the *Titanic* had stopped sending distress calls to the *Virginian* and other ships in the area, she must have gone down already. Van Anda and his staff worked diligently the rest of the night. The next day, readers of the *New York Times* faced a chilling headline:

"New Liner *Titanic* Hits an Iceberg; Sinking by the Bow at Midnight; Women Put Off in Life Boats."

AGONIZING WAIT

Torn between hope and fear, friends and relatives of those aboard the *Titanic* were frantic for information. They swarmed the newspaper office and the headquarters of the White Star Line in New York and in London. Philip Franklin did his best to ease the panic. He tried to dismiss reports of the *Titanic*'s sinking as mere rumors. But inevitably, he received confirmation of the dreaded news. Three-quarters of an hour passed before Franklin could steel himself to meet the public. Later, he wept as he acknowledged "a horrible loss of life."

THE STREETS AROUND THE DOCK IN NEW YORK CITY *are filled with people waiting for the* Carpathia *to arrive with the survivors of the* Titanic. *Although many were looking for loved ones, others were souvenir hunters. In the confusion surrounding the docking, people stripped the lifeboats of oars and life vests and even the nameplates affixed to the bows of the boats. A nameplate and a flag from one of the lifeboats sold at a 1998 Christie's auction for $79,500.*

The frenzy at the White Star offices grew as people tried to find out if their loved ones had been saved. Police had to be called to control the crowd in New York.

CARPATHIA'S ARRIVAL

The terrible wait lasted until Thursday night, April 18, when the *Carpathia* finally arrived in New York. Thirty thousand people stood in the wind and rain to watch the ship dock in Pier 54. Even though the names of the survivors had been wired ahead, people hoped desperately that the list had been incomplete. They called out names as they strained for glimpses of family or friends. The darkness and mass of people made it difficult to spot familiar faces. Arthur Woolcott, expecting to meet his fiancée, Marion Wright, as she exited the ship, finally left sorrowfully without her. His ordeal would end the next day when they were joyfully reunited. But few people who missed seeing their friends or relatives that night enjoyed such a happy outcome.

HAROLD BRIDE'S ORDEAL

Although many reporters covered the *Carpathia*'s arrival in New York, no paper provided better coverage than the *New York Times*. Ignoring expected protocol, editor Carr Van Anda sent sixteen reporters to the scene, four times as many as any other paper. But the paper's biggest coup was landing an interview with the *Titanic*'s wireless operator, Harold Bride *(shown in photo at right as he is helped off the* Carpathia*)*. In a moving statement, Bride honored the musicians who had continued to play as the ship sank. He also praised his fellow wireless operator, Jack Phillips, who remained at his post after the captain released him and who died aboard collapsible boat B.

Bride told of being washed overboard and trapped under a boat and of being pulled onto an overturned collapsible, where his feet were bent out of shape from the weight of another passenger. After three hours aboard the *Carpathia*, Bride was told that the ship's exhausted wireless operator, Harold Cottam, needed help. Personal messages that survivors wanted to send to their loved ones had begun to pile up. "I could not walk," Bride told the reporter. "Both my feet were broken or something, I don't know what. I went on crutches with somebody helping me. I took the [telegraph] key and I never left the wireless cabin after that. Our meals were brought to us. We kept the wireless working all the time."

Bride was still sending messages when *New York Times* reporter Jim Speers, accompanied by Guglielmo Marconi, often considered the inventor of the wireless, arrived to speak with him. The interview has long been hailed as a standard of excellence in journalism. Taken as a whole, the *Times*'s extensive coverage of the *Titanic* disaster helped transform a struggling newspaper into one of the world's most respected publications.

THE *MACKAY-BENNETT'S* SORROWFUL MISSION

The first of several ships sent to recover bodies from the *Titanic*'s last known position, the *Mackay-Bennett* set out from Halifax, Canada, two days after the disaster. The crew found 306 bodies, floating in their life jackets. They had frozen to death in the icy water. Their stopped watches marked the time of the tragedy between 2:00 and 2:20 A.M. John Jacob Astor, who had seen his pregnant wife safely into a lifeboat, was found among the victims. Bodies that could not be recognized were buried at sea. The rest were taken back to Halifax where three cemeteries set aside areas for *Titanic* victims. About fifty-nine bodies were taken elsewhere for burial. Three other ships would follow the *Mackay-Bennett*, but few additional bodies were recovered. As late as the end of June 1912, however, people on steamers passing through the area reported spotting bodies in the water.

SENATOR SMITH'S MISSION

Titanic's passengers, still coming down the gangplank, encountered a busy man jostling against them to board the ship. Senator William Alden Smith was not related to the *Titanic*'s Edward Smith. However, Senator Smith had sailed under the late captain and admired him a great deal. He could not believe the charges that newspapers had begun to raise against Captain Smith. The man the Michigan senator had sailed with had *not* lacked judgment and was *not* more concerned with speed than safety. Senator Smith was determined to learn what really caused the ship to sink. As Smith advanced briskly onto the ship, the U.S. Senate had already passed a resolution to bring together an investigating committee. Spying one of the *Carpathia*'s officers, Smith introduced himself and asked to be taken to Bruce Ismay at once.

Ismay was a broken man. Trembling and unkempt, he could not meet Smith's gaze. Smith, however, was in no mood to mince words. He had learned that Ismay wanted the *Titanic*'s surviving crew members to return home as soon as possible. Such a mass departure would interfere with Smith's investigation and perhaps make it impossible to get at the truth.

MICHIGAN SENATOR WILLIAM ALDEN SMITH *rushed to New York City to begin the* Titanic *Senate inquiry when he found out that J. Bruce Ismay had requested that he and the survivors of the* Titanic *crew be picked up by a White Star ship,* Cedric, *to be immediately returned to England.*

Automatically, Senator Smith launched into his carefully rehearsed speech. "I am empowered by the Congress of the United States to demand that you refrain from leaving my country until my committee has the opportunity to question you about the events surrounding the sinking of the *Titanic*. If necessary, I will issue a subpoena [order to appear in court as a witness] to detain you."

The subpoena proved unnecessary. Senator Smith relaxed after Ismay promised to be present and to contribute whatever he could to the hearings. The two men shook hands. Then Smith returned to the deck where he could observe the joy and pain of the crowds of people on the pier below. Deeply moved, he felt he owed the *Titanic* survivors as well as the victims and their loved ones a full explanation of what had gone wrong.

DURING THE SIX WEEKS OF TESTIMONY, *a total of eighty-two witnesses testified about ice warnings that were ignored, the inadequate number of lifeboats, the ship's speed, the failure of nearby ships to respond to the Titanic's distress calls, and the treatment of passengers of different classes.*

CHAPTER SEVEN

A LEGACY OF SAFETY

Senator Smith wasted no time. The very next day—April 19—he opened his official Senate inquiry by calling Bruce Ismay to the stand. After speaking about the *Titanic*'s sea trials, speed, and propeller revolutions, Ismay concluded, "I was in bed, asleep, when the accident happened. The ship sank, I am told, at two-twenty. That, sir, I think is all I can tell you."

Smith was not about to let his witness off so easily. What had Ismay done after the collision? he wanted to know. On and on the questions went. By the time Smith was done, Ismay had given fifty-eight pages of testimony. The hearings would continue for weeks, eventually being transferred from New York City to Washington, D.C.

BRITISH RESENTMENT

While the majority of the passengers aboard the *Titanic* were American, the officers, the crew, and the staff were almost all British. As the American investigation went forward, resentment against the proceedings flared in Britain. Many British subjects felt that a U.S. court of inquiry should have no power to call British officers and crew members to account. Polish-born British novelist Joseph Conrad summed up the prevailing mood in the literary journal *English Review:* "Why an officer of the British merchant service should answer the questions of any king, emperor, autocrat, or senator of any foreign power (as to an event in which a British ship alone was concerned, and which did not even take place in the territorial waters of that power) passes my understanding." Second Officer Charles Lightoller, who received a grueling interrogation from Smith, would later write, "With all the goodwill in the world, the 'Enquiry' could be called nothing but a complete farce." The British press also complained about the American inquiry. "The Senate committee is not a body of experts," asserted the *London Daily Mail*. The *London Daily Express* dismissed Smith as "a backwoodsman from Michigan."

DIFFERENT APPROACHES

Ignoring British criticism, Smith continued to call crew members and to ask hard questions. After interrogating eighty-two witnesses, the Senate committee criticized Captain Smith for sailing too quickly through ice-infested waters. But since the captain had not broken any maritime [relating to matters of the sea] laws, he was not held responsible for the *Titanic*'s fate. In the final analysis, said the committee members, the ship's fate had to be considered an "Act of God." They signaled out Captain Rostron "as deserving of the highest praise and worthy of especial recognition." But Captain Lord's conduct was deemed "most reprehensible [blameworthy]." Because he was not on trial, the captain could do nothing to refute the finding.

When the British inquiry, conducted by John Charles Bigham (better known as Lord Mersey), began in London on May 2, 1912, Captain Lord had to face more pointed and difficult questions. Since he knew that his officers had seen rockets, why didn't he take action? Why didn't he at least wake up the wireless operator to see if he could find something out? Not surprisingly, Lord's replies failed to satisfy most of his listeners. Like the Americans, the British criticized Lord and praised Rostron.

ISMAY
UNDER FIRE

Even before the *Carpathia* landed in New York, Bruce Ismay was widely criticized. People questioned why the high-ranking White Star official survived while so many others lost their lives. "Ismay could certainly not be held responsible for the collision with the iceberg," said noted admiral Alfred Mahan in the *New York Times*, "but the shortage of lifeboats meant that so long as there was a soul that could be saved, the obligation lay on Mr. Ismay that that one person and not he should have been in the boat."

After answering questions before the Senate committee *(shown in photo at right, Ismay at center)*, Ismay felt it necessary to issue a statement to correct "the untrue statements made in some of the newspapers." He denied saying that the *Titanic* should speed up to get beyond the field of ice more quickly. He also tried to clarify the circumstances of his entering a lifeboat, giving the name of a passenger who could verify his claims. "I hope," he wrote, "I need not say that neither Mr. Carter nor myself would for one moment have thought of getting into the boat if there had been any women there to go in it, nor should I have done so if I had thought that by remaining on the ship I could have been of the slightest further assistance."

Despite the statement and Ismay's full cooperation with both the British and American investigations, the taint associated with his name never lifted. In later years, he could not bear for anyone to mention the *Titanic* in his presence. His wife would lament that the *Titanic* had ruined their lives.

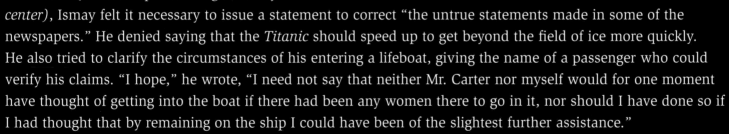

Although Captain Smith had been sailing too fast, he had merely been following established practice. In the eyes of the investigation, Smith made a "mistake," but he could not be held guilty of "negligence." Assigning blame was not as crucial as preventing further tragedies. "The importance of this Inquiry has to do with the future," declared Lord Mersey. "No one can repair the past."

Author and *Titanic* expert Walter Lord later wrote that the American and British inquiries had distinctly different approaches. The British emphasized technical failures such as inadequate lifeboat regulations, unsafe speed, competition between companies, and imperfections in the design of the ship itself. While not ignoring these issues, the American investigation tended to stress the "human" factor. How were the passengers notified of the collision? Why were different procedures followed in the way lifeboats were loaded on the starboard and port sides? Did the three classes of passengers have equal access to the ship's deck?

SAFETY RECOMMENDATIONS

Despite their different approaches, the two investigations came to the same conclusions. Both recommended that all ships carry enough lifeboats to hold everyone on board. Both stressed the need for frequent lifeboat

JOHN CHARLES BIGHAM, KNOWN AS LORD MERSEY, *conducted the British inquiry in May 1912 into the* Titanic *sinking. Some people felt that he was biased toward the Board of Trade and the major shipping companies and was not appropriately concerned about finding out why the ship sank.*

drills and around-the-clock wireless operators. Structural features endorsed by the American and British hearings included "a double skin for the hull, longitudinal [running from bow to stern rather than across] bulkheads and water-tight decks." A minor difference between the two reports concerned the use of searchlights. While the Americans felt that searchlights could prove helpful in detecting icebergs, the British concluded they would be of little use. According to the British findings, additional lookouts would provide a greater measure of safety than searchlights.

DID LIGHTOLLER LIE?

In his testimony before the Senate committee, Charles Lightoller *(right)* said he had not discussed the cause of the accident with Captain Smith or with any of the other senior officers before the ship went down. However, in 2010, his granddaughter, British writer Louise Patten, made a startling claim that contradicted his words. According to Patten, her grandfather knew the real reason the *Titanic* sank. She said that an easily avoidable steering mistake was responsible for the disaster. A misinterpretation of orders at a time when mariners (sailors) were adjusting from sail-powered ships to steam-powered ships caused the person at the wheel to turn the ship in the wrong direction. If he had steered in the correct direction, the ship would have missed the iceberg.

The secret has a second part. Patten said that the *Titanic* continued to forge ahead slowly for ten minutes after the impact. Bruce Ismay, not understanding the seriousness of the collision, convinced Captain Smith to follow this unwise course. The forward motion added greatly to pressure in the lower flooding regions of the ship. This caused the ship to sink faster. Had the *Titanic* stopped at once after hitting the iceberg, she would have stayed afloat many hours longer. "The inquiry had to be whitewashed," Patten told the British newspaper the *Telegraph*. "The only person he [Lightoller] told the full story to was his beloved wife Sylvia, my grandmother." Patten said that loyalty to the company prevented Lightoller from telling the truth at both the American and British inquiries.

Lightoller's family kept the secret for many years to preserve his reputation. But Patten felt it was time to tell the truth and promised to reveal the true nature of the *Titanic* disaster in her forthcoming novel, *Good as Gold*. Why did she decide to disclose the truth in a work of fiction? "I was plotting my second novel and it struck me that I was the last person alive to know what really happened on the night *Titanic* sank," she explained.

LASTING LEGACY: ICE PATROL

Even as the American and British inquiries looked back at the devastating loss, the United States and other governments were looking forward to prevent future disasters. Almost immediately the U.S. Navy delegated two scout cruisers, the *Chester* and the *Birmingham*, to patrol the northwest Atlantic Ocean, especially the area where the *Titanic* went down. The cruisers warned nearby ships of icy conditions, allowing them to change course, if necessary. The next year, the Revenue Cutter Service took over the job. When the first International Convention for the Safety of Life at Sea was held in November 1913, ice patrol was a key topic of discussion. The major seagoing nations—including the United Kingdom, France, Germany, and the United States— as well as other countries agreed to form an International Ice Patrol (IIP). The United States accepted responsibility for the service, with twelve other countries contributing funds for its maintenance.

WAS THE *CALIFORNIAN* TO BLAME?

Censured by both the Americans and the British, Captain Lord never recovered his reputation. Shortly after the inquiries, he resigned. Years later, the discovery of the *Titanic* on the ocean floor brought new evidence to light. In transmitting distress calls over the wireless, Jack Phillips had sent inaccurate coordinates. The ship was not located in the position he had indicated. This raised new issues about the *Californian*'s level of responsibility. In 1990 the Marine Accident Investigation Branch, an agency of the British government, reopened the case of the *Californian*'s conduct in the *Titanic* disaster.

After two years, Deputy Chief Inspector James De Coverly issued a report that officially absolved Captain Lord of blame. According to the document, the *Californian* was probably 17 to 20 miles (27 to 32 km) from the *Titanic*. Although the *Titanic* was probably not seen by the *Californian*'s officers, its distress signals were. The *Californian* should have taken measures to investigate these signals, but the fault lay with Second Officer Herbert Stone rather than Captain Lord. De Coverly summed up the findings: "I do not think any reasonably probable action by Captain Lord could have led to a different outcome to the tragedy. This of course does not alter the fact that the attempt should have been made."

WHAT ABOUT THIRD CLASS?

The guiding principle behind the evacuation of the *Titanic* was "Women and children first." But statistics show that many women and children were lost. Ninety-one women and fifty-five children in third class died. Taken as a whole, only 25 percent of third-class passengers survived as opposed to 63 percent of first-class and 43 percent of second-class passengers. What accounted for this discrepancy? Did class distinction prevail even as the ship was going down? Both the American and British investigations found that no such discrimination existed. But they seem to have ignored a good deal of evidence to the contrary.

During the voyage, third-class passengers were rigidly excluded from first-class areas. These included the boat deck. Olaus Abelseth and Daniel Buckley, two third-class survivors who testified at the U.S. hearing, described the difficulties their fellow steerage passengers had in reaching the boat deck as the ship was sinking. Although Buckley stated at first that no one tried to stop third-class passengers from reaching the lifeboats, his next words turned that statement upside down. "They tried to keep us down at first on the steerage deck," he said. "They did not want us to go up to the first class place at all."

Buckley went on to describe a scene he witnessed in which a crew member stopped a third-class passenger who had passed through a gate into the first-class area. Enraged, the passenger broke the lock and began chasing the crew member. He yelled that if he got his hands on the man, he "would throw him into the water." The passenger's behavior heartened others in third-class who began pouring through the gate. "They [the crew] couldn't keep them [third-class passengers] down," Buckley noted.

At the British inquiry, crew member William Lucas gave one explanation for the few numbers of steerage passengers on the boat deck. "I do not think those people had time to go there without directions from somebody;" he said. "I hardly knew the way there myself." John Hart, one of the stewards for third class, told of conducting a number of women and children through the maze of ship's corridors to the boat deck. However, his statement implied that men wanting to reach the boat deck were prevented from doing so. It seems that both inquiries were more concerned with why the *Titanic* sank than with why a disproportionate number of their second- and third-class passengers died.

In 1914 the Revenue Cutter Service and the ice patrol merged to become the U.S. Coast Guard. Besides monitoring ice, the Coast Guard operates weather stations, enforces international maritime laws, and generally promotes safety on the sea. Its service has only been interrupted by World War I and World War II (1939–1945). Because of the Coast Guard, no ship has been lost due to ice in the North Atlantic since the *Titanic*.

MEMORIALS

Shocked cities in Britain and the United States lost little time in erecting memorials to individuals and to groups of people who died on the *Titanic*. The hardest hit town was Southampton, England, home to a large number of the ship's crew. The bustling port dedicated separate memorials to the engineers, the musicians, and the postal workers as well as another for the stokers, sailors, and stewards who had died. Liverpool, England, home base to the White Star

THIS MEMORIAL IN SOUTHAMPTON, ENGLAND, *is a memorial to the* Titanic *engineers.*

Line, also suffered greatly and constructed several memorials. Important U.S. sites include the Women's Titanic Memorial in Washington, D.C.; the Titanic Memorial Lighthouse in New York City; and the Harry Elkins Widener Memorial Library in Cambridge, Massachusetts.

TITANIC SURVIVORS, *shown here on the* Carpathia, *dealt with the tragedy they had seen and endured in different ways.*

CHAPTER EIGHT

LIFE AFTER THE *TITANIC*

The United **States and Britain issued their reports** on the *Titanic* disaster at the end of May and July, respectively. But the documents did not bring closure to the *Titanic* survivors. Images of the disaster continued to haunt them as they struggled to get on with their lives, at their own pace and in their own ways.

Ruth Becker, twelve years old during the disaster, didn't speak of her experience until she retired as a teacher. For many years, her own children didn't even know she had been on the *Titanic*. As an older woman, however, Ruth began attending meetings of the Titanic Historical Society and sharing some memories. In 1990 she summoned the courage for a cruise to Mexico. It was her first ocean voyage since sailing on the *Titanic* seventy-eight years earlier.

Winnie Troutt, who had originally decided not to seek a place in a lifeboat, lived to be one hundred years old and crossed the Atlantic ten more times by ship. Jokingly, she attributed her long life to "[drinking] plenty of whiskey and [keeping] late hours." She had a lively sense of humor, loved an audience, and was always willing to burst into song or to talk about the *Titanic*. In her nineties, she was still ballroom dancing and driving her red Pinto around Hermosa Beach, California. She also had a serious side and a generous nature. "I felt I was saved for something," she wrote in an article, "so I vowed never to quarrel and always be kind to the sick and elderly."

"THE *TITANIC* BABY"

Philip (Filly) Aks, the baby snatched from his mother and reunited with her on the *Carpathia*, was too young to have memories of the *Titanic*. But he also believed that his survival came with a responsibility to help others. He grew up with his two younger siblings in Norfolk, Virginia. As a teenager, he began working with his father, Sam, in the scrap metal business. During World War II, he did everything possible to salvage iron for the war effort. Active in community affairs, he was also president of his synagogue (Jewish house of worship). After the hull of the *Titanic* was discovered on the ocean floor in 1985, he enjoyed talking to reporters.

MARGARET BROWN

It's said that when the *Carpathia* arrived in New York, a reporter asked Margaret Brown how she had managed to survive. "Typical Brown luck," she supposedly replied. "I'm unsinkable." After her death, her life took on legendary status in the 1960s musical *The Unsinkable Molly Brown*. Although her exploits were greatly exaggerated in the Broadway production, the true facts are exciting enough. On the *Titanic* and in the lifeboat, she demonstrated leadership and courage. Aboard the *Carpathia*, she established a committee to help her fellow survivors and raised ten thousand dollars. One of the last to leave the rescue ship in New York, she made sure that all the survivors had someone to meet them and received medical care, if needed. "After being brined, salted, and pickled in mid ocean I am now high and dry" she wrote to her daughter. "I have had flowers, letters and telegrams—people until I am befuddled. They are petitioning Congress to give me a medal. . . . If I must call in a specialist to examine my head it is due to the title of Heroine of the *Titanic*."

As a celebrity, Margaret Brown (no one ever called her Molly) worked hard to keep her social concerns before the public. These included women's rights, workers' rights, education, and historical preservation. Eight years after the *Titanic* disaster, she was on board a ship 700 miles (1,127 km) out to sea on her way to Denmark when fires flared up in the ship's coal bunkers. Although the crew was not able to extinguish the flames, the ship made it safely back to Halifax. Brown used the extra time in the Canadian city to place wreaths on the graves of *Titanic* victims.

FIRSTHAND ACCOUNTS

While some *Titanic* survivors wanted to forget their terrible ordeal, others felt compelled to share their stories. Thirty-four-year-old teacher and widower Lawrence Beesley wrote his first account of the tragedy while he was still aboard the *Carpathia*. When the ship docked in New York, he was thoroughly prepared to answer reporters' questions. For months, he remained in the United States, expanding his narrative into a book. Then he returned home to Britain on a Cunard ship rather than on a White Star liner. Resuming a normal life, he raised a family with his second wife and enjoyed playing golf. But for the rest of his eighty-nine years, he never ventured to sea again. According to his daughter, the one time his family vacationed at the beach, he turned his back on the ocean and sat facing the land.

TITANIC SURVIVOR MARGARET BROWN *was the inspiration for a 1960 Broadway musical and a 1964 movie* The Unsinkable Molly Brown. *A philanthropist and suffragist, Margaret (never known as Molly) tried to correct the misimpressions of the drama but eventually gave up and withdrew from contact with writers, interviewers, or historians.*

Colonel Archibald Gracie, a writer and amateur historian, also wrote a book. He spent months trying to work out the exact sequence of events and the names of the survivors in each lifeboat. Gracie was clinging to the roof of the bridge when the *Titanic* went down. He found himself sucked into a whirlpool and floundered underwater as he tried desperately to swim away. Eventually he came to collapsible boat B. Making his way through dozens of swimmers, he grasped the arm of a crew member and hoisted himself onto the overturned boat. When the collapsible couldn't hold anyone else, Gracie averted his gaze from the water. He couldn't bear to refuse anyone pleading for help.

Gracie never recovered from the hypothermia and injuries he endured in the water. He died on December 4, 1912. It's said that his last words were "We must get them all into the boats." Gracie's book, *The Truth about the Titanic*, was published in 1913, after his death.

Other survivors would also pen accounts through the years. Jack Thayer, who as a teenager jumped from the ship into the water, waited thirty-eight years to tell his story. By then he had become a banker and was married with two sons. Writing may have been one way to deal with disturbing memories. After the death of his son Edward in World War II, Thayer became depressed and committed suicide on September 20, 1945.

CHARLES LIGHTOLLER: BACK TO THE SEA

A sailor through and through, Charles Lightoller became first officer on the *Oceanic* almost immediately after the *Titanic* disaster. In 1914, when World War I broke out, he joined the United Kingdom's Royal Navy as a lieutenant. His bravery and leadership earned him the Distinguished Service Cross and a promotion to commander. In a bizarre twist of fate, his warship, the *Falcon*, collided with another vessel and sank six years to the day after the *Titanic* went down. Lightoller received a new command and continued to perform outstanding service. By the end of the war, he was a full commander, ready to retire from the navy, though not from the sea. Lightoller returned to the White Star Line, but his association with the *Titanic* prevented him from becoming a captain. Disappointed, he resigned after more than twenty years of service.

During World War II, the navy asked for the use of Lightoller's personal yacht, the *Sundowner*, to help in the evacuation of Dunkirk, France. Four hundred thousand Allied troops (mainly British and French) were trapped near the French city between the English Channel (an arm of the Atlantic Ocean) and approaching German enemy troops. Although Lightoller was sixty-six years old, he insisted on going to Dunkirk himself. A fairly small boat, the *Sundowner* had never carried more than twenty-one persons. Nevertheless, Lightoller, together with his son Roger and an eighteen-year-old Sea Scout named Gerald Ashcroft, rescued 130 men. Bombs fell as they recrossed the English Channel from Britain to France. According to legend, a soldier, startled to hear that Lightoller had been on the *Titanic*, thought he might be safer by jumping overboard. Another soldier saw the situation differently. Someone who survived the *Titanic*, he reasoned, was certain to make it across the channel. In fact, the *Sundowner* did arrive safely back in Ramsgate, England, twelve hours after her departure. Lightoller was a hero.

VIOLET JESSOP: THREE-TIME SURVIVOR:

Stewardess Violet Jessop had the distinction of serving on all three of the great ships envisioned by Pirrie and Ismay. She was working aboard the *Olympic* when it collided with the HMS *Hawke* in 1911. Although each ship incurred considerable damage, both made it back to port safely. Undaunted, the plucky twenty-four-year-old signed up for the *Titanic* the next year. As the ship was sinking, an officer ordered her to set an example for women reluctant to board lifeboats. Obediently, she took a seat in lifeboat 16 to prove that it was not dangerous to be lowered from the ship. As the small craft descended toward the water, someone dropped a baby onto her lap. She cared for the child until another woman took over on the *Carpathia*.

When World War I broke out, Jessop became a nurse with the British Red Cross. She was assigned to the third of White Star's great liners, the *Britannic* (formerly the *Gigantic*), which had become a hospital ship. In 1916 the ship hit a mine (an explosive device) laid by the Germans during the war and began to sink rapidly. "I leapt into the water," Jessop recalled in her memoirs, "but was sucked under the ship's keel, which struck my head. I escaped, but years later when I went to my doctor because of a lot of headaches, he discovered I had once sustained a fracture of the skull." Later, Jessop attributed her survival to her thick hair, which cushioned the blow.

After the war, Jessop went right back to work on the *Olympic*. She continued her maritime adventures until World War II. In 1948 she signed up again with the Royal Mail shipping line. She finally retired from the sea at the age of sixty-three.

OTHER CREW MEMBERS: MOVING FORWARD

Like Lightoller, other crew members continued to sail as they picked up the pieces of their lives. Fourth Officer Boxhall, one of the first to assess damage after the collision, served in the British Royal Navy during World War I. Afterward, he returned to sea, sailing on both White Star and other ships. Although he disliked talking about the *Titanic*, Boxhall agreed to become a technical adviser on *A Night to Remember*, a 1958 film about the *Titanic* disaster. When he died in 1967, Boxhall's ashes were scattered in the ocean over the spot where the *Titanic* was believed to have sunk.

Fifth Officer Harold Lowe, who took a lifeboat back to the wreck site to seek survivors, also served in World War I, afterward continuing his career at sea as a civilian. He never received command of his own vessel, almost certainly due to his association with the *Titanic*. That connection also proved a hindrance to lookout Frederick Fleet. After a brief stint on the *Olympic*, he decided that the White Star Line wanted to forget all about the *Titanic*. That included the men who served on her. Signing on with other shipping companies, Fleet continued to work at sea for twenty-four years. When he retired to land, he built ships at the Harland and Wolff yard in Belfast and later

FREDERICK FLEET *spent much of his life at sea fighting the stigma of having been the lookout on the* Titanic. *After the death of his wife, he was in a state of despondency and committed suicide in January 1965. He was buried in a pauper's grave, though the* Titanic *Historical Society collected donations to place a headstone at his grave in 1993.*

became the shore master-at-arms for a shipping company. In his later years, Fleet was reduced to selling newspapers on a corner and died in poverty.

Wireless operator Harold Bride could practice his profession on land or sea. Taking a job as a telegraph technician for a London post office, he gave little thought to another position aboard ship. Then World War I intervened, and he took a job on a steamer. Later, he became the operator on a ferry that made runs across the English Channel.

ON THE STAGE

Scarcely a month after the *Titanic* sank, the first film drama about the disaster—*Saved from the Titanic*—was released. Still recovering from the shock, silent film star and *Titanic* survivor Dorothy Gibson *(right)* was reluctant at first to participate in the project. But, according to the publication *Motion Picture World*, "the beautiful young cinematic star valiantly conquered her own feeling and forged ahead." Gibson cowrote and starred in the fictionalized account. Soon after *Saved from the Titanic* was released, Gibson gave up acting, turning briefly to opera. In 1914 a studio fire destroyed all the known copies of her last movie. Film historians continue to lament the loss.

Jane Quick and her young daughters Winnifred (Winnie) and Phyllis also took to the stage soon after the disaster. Fred Quick, who met his wife and children in New York, took them on a twenty-one-hour train trip to their new home in Detroit, Michigan. It was there that a vaudeville (stage entertainment featuring various kinds of acts) producer persuaded Jane to tell her story at the Palace Theater. Speaking eight times a day, with eight-year-old Winnie and three-year-old Phyllis, Jane Quick made $7.14 per show, a great deal of money at the time. They went on to perform in Michigan towns Grand Rapids and Battle Creek. Audiences responded with deep interest to their presentations. But finally, Jane Quick decided to cut short her "show business" career. "I'm tired of hearing myself talk," she explained.

In 1922 Bride decided to move to Scotland. The tenth anniversary of the *Titanic* disaster was approaching. Bride did not want any part of the publicity this milestone was sure to generate. In Scotland he lived in happy obscurity with his wife and children. Although he worked as a traveling sales representative, he always made time for his true vocation—telegraphy and radio.

"LAST LIVING LINK"

Elizabeth Gladys "Millvina" Dean was only nine weeks old when she set sail with her parents and older brother as third-class passengers on the *Titanic*. Although she couldn't remember her father, she always credited him with saving her life. "So many other people thought the *Titanic* would never sink," she said in an interview late in her life, "and they didn't bother [to seek a lifeboat]. My father didn't take a chance." After seeing his wife and children safely into a lifeboat, Bertram Dean went down with the ship. Shortly after her arrival in New York, Georgette Dean abandoned her husband's dream of living in the United States. Returning to Southampton, England, she could scarcely bear to speak of the tragedy.

Through the years, Millvina didn't talk much about her family's connection to the *Titanic*. She lived an ordinary life, working for the British government during World War II and later for the purchasing department of an engineering company. "Nobody knew about me and the *Titanic*," she recalled, "to be honest, nobody took any interest, so I took no interest either." Then Millvina got caught in the surge of interest following the discovery of the *Titanic* on the ocean floor. She attended conventions and gave radio and television interviews. She cheerfully obliged the hordes of autograph seekers

MILLVINA DEAN, LAST LIVING *TITANIC* SURVIVOR, *is shown here at a Titanic exhibition at the Maritime Museum in Southampton, England, in 2002. Only nine weeks old when the Titanic sank, she lived to the age of ninety-seven.*

who approached her—especially the children. Asked if she minded presenting the same account over and over, Millvina replied, "Oh not at all. I like it because everyone makes such a fuss of me! And I have traveled so many places because of it, meeting all the people. Oh I wouldn't get tired of it. I'm not the type."

The last of the survivors, Millvina died on May 31, 2009, at the age of ninety-seven. It was the ninety-eighth anniversary of the launching of the *Titanic*. Charles Hass, president of the Titanic International Society, praised her as a "remarkable, sparkling lady" and mourned the passing of "the last living link to the story."

MANY PEOPLE WANTED TO FIND THE *TITANIC*
on the ocean floor where it sank, but it took more than half a century
before a discovery was made.

CHAPTER NINE

QUEST FOR THE *TITANIC*

As the survivors strove to go on with their lives, another story of the *Titanic* was already beginning—the search to find and perhaps to raise the ship. Almost immediately after the disaster, Vincent Astor, who believed his father's body was trapped inside the ship, suggested finding and exploding the hull. That way he believed the body might be recovered. He abandoned the plan when his father's body was discovered the next day. Later in the year, however, he joined with the Widener and Guggenheim families in hiring a wrecking company to locate and recover the hull. Given the technology of the day, this proved to be an impossible task. But two years later, the magazine *Popular Mechanics*, confident in scientific progress, declared that someday explorers would find the wreck and photograph it.

FANCIFUL SCHEMES

Through the years, some imaginative ideas were put forth for raising the *Titanic*. Denver architect Charles Smith suggested attaching electromagnets to a submarine and to the *Titanic*'s hull. The ship would be drawn to the submarine, and cables could be used to hoist the *Titanic* from the sea. An even more original scheme would involve fastening pontoons (portable floats) to the wreck that would then float the hull up to the surface. Neither proposal was tried.

With the advent of World War I, interest in the *Titanic* faded. Then came the Great Depression (1929–1942) and World War II. Occupied with grave matters, most people had little thought to spare for the *Titanic*. Finally, in the 1950s, the ill-fated vessel began to seep into the public awareness again. Two things contributed to the resurgence of interest. A British salvage firm tried and failed to find the wreck. And in 1955, author Walter Lord published his powerful and popular account of the tragedy titled *A Night to Remember*. The movie that soon followed Lord's acclaimed book further kindled people's enthusiasm. They began to ask questions. Where was the ship? Why did it go down? Could it have been saved? Would it ever be found?

A British adventurer named Douglas Woolley put forth some far-fetched ideas to raise the ship that involved water-filled plastic containers and nylon balloons. He generated a fair amount of publicity, but not enough money to move forward with his plans. Still ideas continued to proliferate. Someone wanted to freeze the ship's interior. This was supposed to make it float to the surface in the way that ice always floats to the surface. Another dreamer thought a nitrogen-filled net draped around the ship would do the same job. One would-be explorer envisioned filling the hull with Ping-Pong balls. What about molten wax? A *Titanic* buff proposed infusing 180,000 tons (163,292 metric tons) of melted wax into the ship. Once the wax hardened, the hull should float to the surface.

JACK GRIMM

A serious obstacle to every scheme was that no one knew exactly where the *Titanic* lay. In 1980 Jack Grimm, a colorful Texas millionaire, decided to remedy that situation. The intrepid adventurer had previously launched expeditions in search of the fabled Loch Ness Monster in Scotland, the legendary Big Foot of the Pacific Northwest, and the biblical Noah's Ark. Grimm spared no expense in recruiting his team, which included a film producer, two world-renowned oceanographers from New York's Columbia University, and thirty-six other scientists.

His chartered vessel had state-of-the-art sonar equipment and underwater cameras. Despite these advantages, the mission failed due to bad weather and technological difficulties. Refusing to give up, Grimm mounted two more expeditions in 1981 and 1983. But even with naval vessels and navigational equipment from the U.S. National Aeronautics and Space Administration (NASA), he couldn't locate the wreckage. Although he believed he might have located a propeller, Grimm had no evidence to back it up.

ROBERT BALLARD: YOUNG OCEANOGRAPHER

Unlike Grimm, Robert Ballard was an experienced marine geologist. Long before he even thought of the *Titanic*, the ocean fascinated him. Growing up in the seaside city of San Diego, California, he loved to stroll along the beach and explore tide pools. He even likened himself to the fictional character Robinson Crusoe, discovering "adventure washed up on [the] shore." Young Ballard enjoyed reading adventure books and the science fiction novels of Jules Verne. Captain Nemo, the hero of Verne's *20,000 Leagues Under the Sea*, especially intrigued him. Nemo had created his own submarine. What better adventure could an ocean-loving boy imagine?

FAR FROM BEING A TREASURE HUNTER, ROBERT BALLARD *was a legitimate marine explorer with a stellar record. His first graduate degree (M.S., 1966) was in geophysics from the University of Hawaii. He began his Ph.D. in marine biology at the University of California but was called to active military duty before finishing it. After leaving the U.S. Navy in 1970, he earned a Ph.D. in marine geology and geophysics at the University of Rhode Island.*

Walter Lord's *A Night to Remember* also enthralled Ballard. In his mind, he pictured the splendors of the grand staircase and the ornate chandeliers, forever hidden underwater. Could the majestic ship ever be found? Young Ballard began to dream of it.

ARGO AND *JASON*

Many years later, as a young scientist at the Woods Hole Oceanographic Institution in Massachusetts, Ballard obtained naval funding to develop an undersea exploring system. Excitedly, he assembled a top-notch team of scientists to work on the project, designated the Deep Submergence Laboratory. Ballard aimed to design a remote-controlled unmanned robot to be lowered into the ocean while cabled to a ship on the surface. Scientists on the ship would collect the information and data transmitted by the robot. The navy needed such a system to investigate the wreckage of two nuclear-powered submarines, the *Thresher* and the *Scorpion*. The situation was especially critical because the *Scorpion* contained two nuclear-tipped torpedoes. It was imperative to know what happened to them. Did they pose a danger to the environment or to passing ships? Ballard realized that the robotic device would be perfect for another mission as well—finding the *Titanic*.

ROBERT BALLARD DESIGNED A NUMBER OF DEEP-SEA EXPLORATION VESSELS, *among them the* Argo, *a 16-foot (5 m) submersible sled fitted with a remote-controlled camera that could transmit live images to a monitor anywhere in the world.*

Tackling the job energetically, the Woods Hole team came up with two mechanisms for undersea exploring. Ballard dubbed them *Argo* and *Jason*. In Greek mythology, Jason sailed on a ship named *Argo* in search of the Golden Fleece, an extremely valuable prize. The submersible (underwater exploration vessel) *Argo*, in Ballard's system, would be lowered from a surface ship to the ocean floor. When something merited further investigation, the robotic *Jason* would emerge from *Argo* to gather data—what Ballard called "modern science's equivalent of the Golden Fleece."

A year before *Jason* was ready, *Argo* got its test run in an underwater exploration of the submarine *Thresher*. Analyzing the data, Ballard observed the interesting way in which debris from the wreck had spread across the ocean floor. "The pattern," he would write later, "resembled a comet and its tail."

DEBRIS

In 1985 the *Argo* was put to work again, this time exploring the *Scorpion*. The navy allotted three weeks to investigate the wreckage. To Ballard's delight, the submarine and its debris field were completely mapped within only four days. That meant that Ballard could use the remaining time to pursue his long-delayed dream of finding the *Titanic*. Joining forces with a French exploring group, L'Institut Français de Recherche pour l'Exploration de la Mer (IFREMER), he set off in the vessel *Knorr* toward the coordinates at which the *Titanic* was thought to have sunk. Remembering the lesson from the *Thresher*, he was determined to look for debris. Finding the debris field would surely lead him straight to the ship itself.

"WRECKAGE"

The challenge proved more difficult than Ballard had anticipated. Days passed while *Argo* transmitted nothing but featureless pictures of the ocean floor. Crew members, ever more discouraged, took four-hour stints at the consoles, monitoring every image and fighting boredom. Then, in the early hours of September 1, 1985, an object appeared on the screen. Instantly alert, the team studied it carefully. It seemed to be a piece of twisted steel. "Wreckage!" cried someone.

Excitement mounted as more objects began to appear on the monitor—pipes, pieces of plating, deck railings, and portholes. Then a large, round disk—what looked like a giant boiler—came across the screen. Jean-Louis Michel, the head of the French team, hurried to locate some early photos of the *Titanic*'s construction in the Belfast shipyard. An old picture of

ROBERT BALLARD AND HIS TEAM ABOARD THE *KNORR* consult *charts as they search for the wreckage of the* Titanic.

an enormous boiler looked exactly like the one on the screen. There could be no more doubt. The American-French expedition had found the *Titanic*.

The crew broke out in noisy celebration. Meanwhile, the ship's cook summoned Ballard, who had been resting in his cabin. "Uh, the guys think you should come down to the van," he said. Hurriedly putting on a jumpsuit over his pajamas, Ballard raced to the monitoring area. Amid the happy commotion, a single word jumped out at him—"boiler."

"SHE'S UPRIGHT"

It was about 2:00 A.M. The team members were still reeling from their success when someone remarked, "You know, she sinks in twenty minutes," recalling that the *Titanic* had gone down at 2:20 A.M. The sobering reminder changed the focus from victory to tragedy. Instinctively, the crew gathered on deck for a moment of silent tribute. Ballard raised the flag of the White Star Line over a calm sea. When the short service ended, he thanked the crew and declared, "Now let's get back to work."

After a day of ceaseless activity and explorations, it was time to send the *Argo* over the *Titanic* itself. Eagerly the crew members gathered around the monitors as *Argo* approached the area where they

EMOTIONAL RESPONSE

Even decades later, the fate of the *Titanic* still has the power to overwhelm people. Robert Ballard was surprised by his own feelings. "When I first set out after the *Titanic*, it was sort of a mechanical, technical problem," he has recalled. "My soul was not in it. My mind was in it." That changed completely when the ship was discovered. "It blew me right away," he said, "like a truck ran over the top of me. It was months before I could deal with it emotionally."

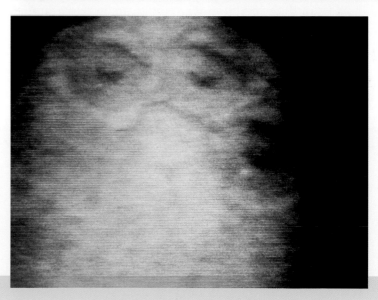

THIS FIRST IMAGE OF THE RIVETS AND FIRE DOORS *showed the crew that they had found the boiler of the* Titanic.

believed the *Titanic* lay. What must have seemed like endless moments passed before the monitor showed a faint image of a huge wall. "It's the side of the ship!" cried Ballard. "She's upright!" Breathlessly, the crew watched as the submersible passed over the port side of the boat deck where they noted a funnel was gone. Then the *Argo* moved across the bridge to the starboard side where a boat davit loomed into view.

When the *Argo* completed its six-minute sweep of the wreckage, the crew noisily gave vent to their enthusiasm. "People were whooping, hugging, and dancing around," Ballard wrote later. But the two leaders of the expedition were too overcome to join the commotion. "As the celebrations continued around us, Jean-Louis and I were almost in tears," recalled Ballard. "Perhaps we were—I don't remember."

More discoveries were in store. On *Argo*'s third pass over the hull, those on duty were startled and dismayed to find the stern missing. Another underwater device, the ANGUS (Acoustically Navigated Geophysical Underwater Survey) had also been dispatched to take photos. When the first images from ANGUS turned our poorly, Ballard sent the submersible out again despite rising winds and rough waters. This time the results proved well worth the effort. The images were sharp and vivid, revealing many details.

A "QUIET AND PEACEFUL" PLACE

Even before the *Knorr* reached Woods Hole, pictures from the expedition were broadcast in the United States. The crew received a gala welcome when the ship arrived back on September 9. A band, swarms of people, flags, and a cannon salute were the last things Ballard had expected. Sudden elevation to celebrity status took him completely by surprise.

MISUNDERSTANDING

Despite an agreement that photos from the 1985 expedition in search of the *Titanic* would be released simultaneously in the United States and in France, a misunderstanding caused American television to broadcast the images first. This would lead to hard feelings between the American and French team members and an end to the collaboration between the Woods Hole Oceanographic Institution and IFREMER on matters relating to the recovery of the *Titanic*.

In a prepared statement, John-Louis Michel stressed that the quest for *Titanic* had been conducted "with her dignity in mind at all times." Similarly mindful of those who had died, Ballard described the ship as it lay in 13,000 feet (3,962 m) of water. "It is a quiet and peaceful and fitting place for the remains of this greatest sea tragedies to rest," he said. "May it forever remain that way and may God bless these found souls."

SECOND EXPEDITION

A year passed before Ballard had the opportunity to return to the *Titanic*. "The longest year of my life," he would later call it. His second expedition, encompassing fifty-six crew members aboard the naval vessel *Atlantis II*, set off in July 1986. This time the ship carried a three-person submersible named *Alvin* and the newest deep-sea exploring robot, *Jason Jr.*, or *J. J.* Ballard did not place much faith in the future of manned, deep-sea vehicles. On several occasions, he had publicly compared them to "dinosaurs headed for extinction." Despite his view, nothing was going to stop him from seeing the *Titanic* in person. On July 13, he joined crew members Ralph Hollis and Dudley Foster in the submersible's first descent to the ship's resting place. Crammed into a sphere just 6 feet (1.8 m) across, the men had little room to move as *Alvin*

ROBERT BALLARD SAID OF HIS ANGUS DEVICE, *"Initially, it was sort of a wind-up toy. You wound up this camera so to speak, and it could take 16,000 photographs at one lowering. I would drop it down, and then for 12 to 14 hours, I would tow it through the valley, bring it up, process all the film, and then look at all the pictures. All those images were my windows into the deep sea."*

went downward at about 1 mile (1.6 km) per hour. Ballard noted a jellyfish and then a white-tipped shark outside his viewing porthole.

Daylight vanished quickly as the submersible continued its descent. Halfway to the ocean bed, a shrill alarm startled the men from their reveries. A battery pack had become contaminated with seawater. They had a backup pack, but they would have to drastically shorten their time on the ocean floor.

"WALL OF STEEL"

The alarms continued to go off as the submersible took on water. The seepage was beginning to short-circuit the batteries. The sonar and tracking weren't working. "Look, we're going to have to abort [stop the dive]," the pilot announced.

Ballard's nerves were strained to the breaking point. "No! No, no, no. Come on!" he cried. "I've waited so long for this moment. Don't abort the dive."

The pilot continued to descend amid the shrieking alarms. "We've got minutes, Bob," he said as they reached the bottom. "We've got to get out of here."

Ballard was still determined to see the *Titanic*, even though all he spied from his viewing porthole was mud. "Keep going. Speed up, go faster," he urged.

At Ballard's insistence, the pilot took *Alvin* toward some unusual mud formations. Ballard believed the "mud balls" had been thrown up from the ocean floor when the *Titanic* hit. Then the crew came to a tall barrier of mud. Intuitively, Ballard knew what they would find beyond the barrier. As they rounded the corner, the great hull of the *Titanic* loomed suddenly before them.

"There was this wall of steel," Ballard later recalled. "It was big, the end of the universe. It was just there as a statement."

The men had only twelve seconds to gaze in wonder before they were forced to abort the dive. The next day, *Alvin* and the robot *J. J.* were ready to return to duty. Robert descended again with Hollis and a new partner, Martin Bowen. This time the submersible landed on the slanting deck of the bow. Ballard never forgot the moment. "It was clunk, clunk," he recalled. "It was like Armstrong on the moon [referring to the landing of the first man on the moon in 1969]."

For five hours, the rapt crew explored the vessel. The pictures taken in 1985 had suggested that the ship was in excellent condition. Up close, the men could see this wasn't so. A thick layer of orange rust coated the steel hull. Sea creatures called mollusks had bored into the woodwork, consuming almost every last particle.

Ballard and various crew members continued the dives for ten more days. Every day they picked something new to explore, such as the grand staircase, the bow, or the debris field. They found the *Titanic*'s stern on July 22. Unlike the well-preserved bow, the stern had been crushed so that the decks were jammed together. All in all, the expedition gathered an immense amount of information. Yet the story of the *Titanic* was still far from over. "We didn't know it at the time," one of *Alvin*'s pilots, Will Sellers, would recall, "but the *Titanic* was to have many visitors in years to come."

"A MILLION THINGS TO DO"

After Robert Ballard returned from his 1985 expedition, his mother said it was a nice accomplishment, adding, "But it's too bad you found the *Titanic*." Ballard was taken aback until she went on to explain. "You know your father and I are very proud that you and your brother went to college and got doctorates and are great scientists but now they'll only remember you for finding the *Titanic*."

Ballard's mother had a point. Few people outside his field realize the full extent of Ballard's contributions to oceanography. During his career, he has led or been part of more than 120 undersea explorations all over the world. He discovered the British ocean liner *Lusitania*, torpedoed in the Atlantic Ocean in 1915 during World War I. He went on to find the remains of many vessels that were sunk in World War II, including U.S. president John F. Kennedy's *PT-109*, which was hit by an enemy Japanese destroyer in 1943. In 1989 he located the World War II German battleship *Bismarck*, sunk in the Atlantic Ocean 4,000 feet (1,219 m) deeper than the *Titanic*'s resting place.

Looking much farther into the past, Ballard led the first deep-sea archaeological mission in 1997. Heading for the Mediterranean Sea on the *NR-1*, a nuclear research submarine belonging to the U.S. Navy, Ballard's team aimed to explore a particularly intriguing debris field.

Their investigations revealed a series of ancient cargo ships spanning the time frame from the first century B.C. through the fourth century A.D. In 2000 Ballard and his team went on to discover what television news program *60 Minutes* called "the best preserved ancient shipwreck ever discovered in the deep sea," a fifteen-hundred-year-old wooden vessel in the Black Sea. Ballard explained that this and other wrecks are incredibly well preserved in the Black Sea because of the lack of rust-causing oxygen in the deep portions of this body of water.

Although Ballard is best known for exploring shipwrecks, he has made other scientific breakthroughs. Ballard is especially proud of finding underwater hot thermal springs off the Galápagos Islands in the Pacific Ocean. The discovery of animals living in these springs revised ideas about the conditions necessary for life. Ballard was also part of the first team to explore the mid-ocean-ridge system, which extends over more than 23 percent of Earth's surface.

The author of several books, Ballard created the Jason Project in 1989 to challenge and encourage middle-school students interested in science. "You only come on this planet once," declared Ballard when he was interviewed by the Academy of Achievement. "so I'm trying to live six or seven lives simultaneously. . . . There are a million things to do."

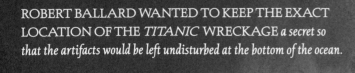

ROBERT BALLARD WANTED TO KEEP THE EXACT LOCATION OF THE *TITANIC* WRECKAGE *a secret so that the artifacts would be left undisturbed at the bottom of the ocean.*

CHAPTER TEN

"THE BIGGEST MUSEUM IN THE WORLD"

After his 1986 exploration, Robert Ballard could have revealed the exact location of the *Titanic*, but he chose not to. He considered the site a sacred memorial and wished to protect it from exploitation. Although initially he supported salvaging artifacts from the wreck, he soon changed his mind. Ballard had come to believe that the *Titanic* should be preserved forever in the state in which it was discovered. Many people agreed with Ballard that the ship's final resting place should be protected. Even the U.S. government became involved. In 1986 Congress passed the Titanic Maritime Memorial Act, a call for the creation of worldwide guidelines to be used for further expeditions. Supporters of the act reasoned that a set of generally accepted principles would help future expeditions to safeguard the "scientific, cultural, and historical significance" of the *Titanic*.

TO SALVAGE OR NOT

Robert Ballard's former French partners at IFREMER disagreed with the explorer on the removal of artifacts. Joining with a team from Connecticut, Titanic Ventures, they revisited the shipwreck in 1987. In addition to scientific investigation, the crew planned to salvage whatever items they could find. Over the course of thirty-two dives in a state-of the-art submersible, the *Nautile*, they recovered eighteen hundred articles from the ship and its debris field. These included brass uniform buttons, luggage, a diamond and sapphire ring, and a statue of a bronze cherub (angel) that had adorned the grand staircase.

A FRENCH COMPANY AND A TEAM FROM THE UNITED STATES LAUNCHED THE *NAUTILE* in 1987 *to recover artifacts from the* Titanic *wreckage.*

Although Ballard voiced strenuous objections to the decision to recover artifacts, he felt that *Titanic* survivor Eva Hart made the most compelling case for leaving the ship alone. As a child, she had watched the ship's stern sink into the ocean, knowing her father was still aboard. Like Ballard, she felt that the best way to honor the memory of those who had died was to leave the *Titanic* in peace.

A retired welfare officer and justice of the peace living near London, Hart felt the salvagers were motivated solely by the profit they would make by public exhibitions of the artifacts. "To bring up those things from a mass sea grave just to make a few thousand pounds shows a dreadful insensitivity and greed," she argued. "The grave should be left alone. They're simply going to do it as fortune hunters, vultures, pirates!"

American political commentator William F. Buckley Jr., who descended in the *Nautile* to view the *Titanic* had a different view of the matter. "You hardly consecrate the artifacts that went down on the *Titanic* by leaving them on the ocean floor," he said.

THE GIANT SCREEN

Public fascination with the *Titanic* continued unabated as more expeditions retrieved artifacts and studied the site. The fourth trip to the shipwreck, a joint Canadian and Soviet project, resulted in a giant screen IMAX film, *Titanica*, in 1995. The remarkable footage gave a vivid impression of encountering the great ship. In addition to filming the site, the crew studied life in the ocean depths. They recorded twenty-four species of animals and four species of fish in the *Titanic*'s vicinity.

ARTIFACTS THAT HAVE BEEN BROUGHT UP *from the* Titanic *include a black purser's bag and its contents.*

UNDERWATER MEMORIALS

Expeditions to the *Titanic* have not only removed artifacts, they have left things there as well. In 1986 Robert Ballard's team left a plaque on the stern in memory of all who died. They also placed one on the bow that entreats future visitors to leave the site undisturbed. When Ballard returned with another expedition in 2004, he discovered several additional plaques *(pictured at right)*. Three honor the Irish victims from Queenstown (renamed Cobh); five postal workers who lost their lives; and the late R. Frank Busby, an expert in submersibles. One of Ballard's own plaques was missing, but nearby he spied a small memorial that had been left by James Cameron the producer-

director of the popular movie, *Titanic*. "The 1,500 souls here still speak," read the inscription, "reminding us always that the unthinkable can happen, but for our vigilance, humility and compassion."

RMS TITANIC, INC.

The Connecticut group that partnered with IFREMER in 1987 eventually grew into a company called RMS Titanic, Inc. Hoping to salvage artifacts for public exhibitions and museums, it spent millions of dollars on its expeditions. Its next step was to bring objects recovered from its 1987 journey into an admiralty, or maritime court, in Norfolk, Virginia. The company gave public notice of its intention to become "salvor in possession" of the *Titanic*. According to maritime law, the first expedition to recover artifacts from a shipwreck in international waters can claim exclusive status when it comes to salvaging any future items. On June 7, 1994, the court upheld the company's claim. This meant that no other organization would be allowed to recover objects from the ship. Other groups, however, could visit the shipwreck to conduct scientific investigations and create documentaries.

An exhibit of items salvaged by RMS Titanic, Inc., opened in London at the National Maritime Museum on October 4, 1994. Included among the artifacts were a chandelier, a champagne bottle, a shaving brush, various small statues, and a porthole. Captain Smith's great-nephew condemned the display as disrespectful to those who went down on the *Titanic*. In contrast, the

TITANIC ARTIFACTS *were on display at the National Maritime Museum in London, England, in October 1994. The exhibit included a porthole, a champagne bottle with its contents intact, a chandelier, crystal, traveler's checks, and a leather cigarette case—complete with cigarettes.*

chairman of the museum's board of trustees stressed that ethical principles had been established to govern this and all future displays of relics.

Titanic survivor Millvina Dean admitted to having two minds about the exhibit. "I was against bringing the artifacts up in the first place," she declared. "I didn't want anything to be touched because I thought my father was there. But once they had brought them up from the seabed, there was nothing anyone could do about it, and I thought people might as well see the things as a part of history."

In 1996, RMS Titanic, Inc. joined forces with the Discovery Channel and a French group on a mission that combined both salvage operations and scientific investigations. The team, which included oceanographers, biologists, metallurgists, naval architects, and recovery experts, would attempt to answer some key questions about the nature of the damage to the *Titanic* and the possibility that faulty construction materials figured in the disaster.

WHAT WAS THE DAMAGE INFLICTED BY THE ICEBERG?

The immediate result of the *Titanic*'s impact with the iceberg surprised some team members. Sonar scanning showed that the *Titanic* had not sustained one continuous gash as had often been assumed. In fact, the damage seemed very slight compared to the size of the ship—six narrow slits, whose area totaled only about 12 square feet (1.1 sq. m). But the slits were 20 feet (6 m) below the waterline. The water pressure was so intense that water began pushing through the openings at an incredible rate. Less than an hour after the collision, 7.5 tons (6.8 metric tons) of water had surged into the ship.

THE BIG PIECE

The pressure exerted on the wreck of the *Titanic* by the ocean is 6,000 pounds per square inch (422 kg-force per sq. cm). Because the ship is in danger of collapsing, it cannot be raised. However, in 1996 RMS Titanic, Inc., brought a section of the hull weighing about 17 to 18 tons (15 to 16 metric tons) to within 200 feet (61 m) of the ocean's surface. A ship attempted to tow what was dubbed "the big piece" to New York. But cables holding the piece could not withstand the fierce winds and violent waves when a hurricane overtook the ship. The big piece sank again to the ocean floor where it remained for two years. Finally, in 1998 RMS Titanic, Inc., raised the piece again and succeeded in bringing it to the United States. It has been displayed in several locations around the country *(shown at right on display in San Francisco, California).*

COULD THE SHIP HAVE BEEN SAVED?

By studying computer models, engineers developed two scenarios in which the *Titanic* might have stayed afloat longer. According to one theory, if the ship had hit the iceberg straight on instead of scraping the side, the bow would have been crushed. People in that part of the ship would have been killed. But the majority of the passengers and the crew members would have lived. The second possibility has to do with the speed of the ship. If the *Titanic* had been going half as fast, she would have had less damage. This would have resulted in less flooding and the possibility that the ship could have reached New York.

DID WEAK STEEL CONTRIBUTE TO THE *TITANIC*'S DISASTER?

The 1996 expedition collected more than 200 pounds (90 kg) of twisted, rusty steel from the *Titanic*'s debris field. A series of tests revealed the presence of manganese sulfide, a compound that lessens the strength of steel, especially in extremely cold temperatures. "More or less," explained materials scientist Timothy Foecke of the National Institute of Standards and Technology in Gaithersburg, Maryland, "when you take the [inferior] steel down to a lower temperature, you're actually shattering something that's full of holes." The poor quality of the steel may have contributed to the *Titanic*'s breakup before it sank.

In 1912 engineers would not have been aware of the importance of the steel's chemical structure. But a 2008 book, *Titanic's Last Secrets* by Brad Matsen, suggests that after the disaster, officials at Harland and Wolff may have realized that the ship's hull wasn't strong enough. Tom McCluskie, a retired archivist at the shipyard, told Matsen about a company investigation that was done after the disaster. According to records, engineers believed that the *Titanic* would have stayed afloat much longer if the steel hull and the rivets used in its construction had been stronger. McCluskie also produced documentation that designer Thomas Andrews had called for steel 1.25 inches (3.2 cm) thick. This exceeded the standard set by the British Board of Trade, which only required 1-inch (2.5 cm) steel. The White Star Line preferred the thinner steel because the ship would be lighter. The Harland and Wolff shipbuilders complied with their wishes. Others argue that if weak steel did contribute to the ship's demise, the ship would have broken apart while it was still low in the water. The steel would probably not have been strong enough to raise the ship to the high angle relative to the water that has been traditionally assumed.

WHAT WILL HAPPEN TO THE *TITANIC*?

After about one hundred years since sinking, the *Titanic* is decomposing at a fairly swift rate. Bacteria and fungi have been feeding off the iron of the hull, as evidenced by the icicle-shaped rusticles that cover the ship. The products these microbes release then become part of the rusticles. Eventually the structure will become so weak that it will simply crumple on the ocean floor.

VIRTUAL MUSEUM

Robert Ballard wants to make the most of the time left before the *Titanic* disintegrates. In 2004, on a return trip to the ship, he broadcast live pictures of his exploration on television. Ballard would like to make such electronic coverage of the site continuous and available over the Internet. The *Titanic* would become a sort of virtual museum, which could be visited any hour of the day or night. "I think the *Titanic*'s critical because people are fascinated by the *Titanic*," Ballard told National Public Radio when he returned from his expedition. "But I'm, if you want to know the truth, far more interested in ancient antiquity. We think the deep sea is a giant museum. We've been finding shipwrecks dating back to the Phoenicians, the Romans, the Greeks—and those ships are at peril." He wants to "use *Titanic* as a platform to present our case that the deep sea is the biggest museum in the world—it has more artifacts in it than all the museums of the world combined, and yet there's no lock on the door.... We need to generate international laws to protect human antiquity."

If Ballard has his way, the *Titanic* may yet change the future of underwater archaeology.

PASSENGERS LINE UP TO GET INTO LIFEBOATS
in a scene from the 1997 movie Titanic *by James Cameron.*

EPILOGUE

THE STORY THAT NEVER GROWS OLD

After Ballard's discovery of the ship in 1985, interest in the *Titanic* skyrocketed. Ballard and subsequent explorers added to the growing volume of *Titanic* literature with books of their own. And Walter Lord, author of the acclaimed *A Night to Remember*, made another contribution with his 1986 book, *The Night Lives On.*

The year 1997 saw the release of the critically acclaimed and popular film, *Titanic.* The desire of producer and director James Cameron to see the shipwreck himself lay behind the making of one of the most popular movies of all time. "I made *Titanic* because I wanted to dive to the shipwreck, not because I particularly wanted to make the movie," he explained. "When I learned some other guys had dived to the *Titanic* to make an IMAX movie, I said, 'I'll make a Hollywood movie to pay for an expedition and do the same thing.'" Footage from his 1995 expedition is interspersed in the film, which moves back and forth between a tragic love story on the ship in 1912 and a modern-day exploration of the wreckage. *Titanic* went on to become the highest-grossing movie of all time, a position it held until 2010.

ANOTHER TRAGEDY

James Cameron's blockbuster hit was not the end of his keen interest in the *Titanic*. He was on the ocean floor, surveying the wreck on September 11, 2001. When he and his colleagues rose to their vessel, the *Keldysh*, and emerged from their submersible, they learned of the terrorist attacks on the World Trade Center in New York and the Pentagon near Washington, D.C. Suddenly exploring the *Titanic* seemed meaningless. But as days passed, they began to realize that the devastating events of what would come to be known as 9/11 did not lessen the tragedy of the *Titanic* or make it irrelevant. Somehow the eighty-nine-year-old disaster helped them deal with their very recent feelings of loss and grief. "Perhaps," Cameron has written, "that is ultimately the reason for our collective fascination with the *Titanic*." He calls the account "the quintessential story of loss,

TITANIC HISTORICAL SOCIETY

Edward Kamuda was a teenager in 1953 when he saw the award-winning film *Titanic*. Fascinated, he began exchanging letters with forty *Titanic* survivors. Finally, some of his correspondents suggested that Kamuda set up a museum. Excited by the idea, he founded the Titanic Historical Society on July 7, 1963. Many survivors donated items for the small museum, which he set up in the back room of his jewelry store in Indian Orchard, Massachusetts. From a few individuals, the organization grew to a membership of several thousand from all over the world.

of coming to terms with death, of heroism and cowardice, and the full spectrum of human response before, during and after a crisis." As days passed, the crew of the *Keldysh* began to find purpose in their work again. The documentary that resulted from their exploration, *Ghosts of the Abyss*, opened in 2003.

TITANIC ARTIST

Like Edward Kamuda, Ken Marschall can date his interest in the *Titanic* to a movie he saw as a teenager. The 1953 movie *Titanic* captivated him so much that he painted his first picture of the ship the night he saw it. After attending Pasadena City College in California, he began his career as a maritime artist. Although he accepted commissions for other ocean liners, he was most often asked to paint the *Titanic (one of his paintings is shown at right)*. In researching the ship, Marschall gathered a vast array of materials and photographs and became a widely sought-after expert. He accompanied James Cameron on his 2001 and 2005 expeditions to the *Titanic*. "His paintings almost seemed to be stills from a movie that hadn't yet been made," Cameron once remarked. "And I thought to myself . . . I can make these paintings live."

One hundred years after the disaster, the *Titanic* continues to intrigue people. New explorations still make headlines. Exhibits draw throngs, eager to see articles salvaged from the wreck. Memorabilia from survivors fetch record prices. Plans are even afoot for a memorial cruise through the same waters on the one-hundredth anniversary of the disaster. A *New York Times* editorial may have put it best. "There is really no getting over the *Titanic*, at least not where the human imagination is concerned."

Perhaps no one will ever know the exact details of what really happened to the *Titanic*. But expeditions will continue to seek answers. Authors and filmmakers will continue to dramatize events. The story of the *Titanic* is both history and news. No matter how many times it is told, it never seems to grow old.

WHAT REALLY HAPPENED?

In 2005 Richie Kohler and John Chatterton, hosts of the History Channel's popular series *Deep Sea Detectives*, joined the select group of explorers who have descended to the *Titanic*. To their astonishment, they found enormous segments of the ship's bottom, resting about 1,500 feet (457 m) from the rest of the wreckage. According to naval architect Roger Long, the discovery drastically alters the scenario of the *Titanic*'s demise. He believes that the ship broke at a low angle to the surface of the water—not the high angle formerly assumed and that is depicted so vividly in James Cameron's *Titanic*. If Long is correct, structural weakness caused the ship to sink sooner than has been generally accepted. Those aboard who expected the *Titanic* to stay afloat in time for a rescue ship to arrive were caught off guard.

TITANIC TIMELINE

1907   Bruce Ismay and Lord James Pirrie decide to build three luxury ships to compete with Britain's Cunard Line.

1911   The *Titanic*'s hull is launched on May 31.

1912   The *Titanic* sets out on its maiden voyage from Southampton, England, on April 10. It nearly collides with the steamer *New York*.

The *Titanic* strikes an iceberg on April 14 at 11:40 P.M. Captain Smith gives orders to load the lifeboats.

The *Titanic* sinks on April 15 at 2:20 A.M.

The *Carpathia* arrives a little over an hour after the *Titanic* goes down.

The *Carpathia* arrives in New York City with the survivors of the *Titanic* on the evening of April 18.

The American inquiry into the disaster is conducted from April 19 through May 18. The British inquiry is held from May 2 through July 3.

1913   The International Ice Patrol is established to warn ships of icy conditions in the North Atlantic Ocean.

1955   Walter Lord's classic book about the sinking of the *Titanic*, *A Night to Remember*, is published.

1960   *The Unsinkable Molly Brown* opens as a Broadway musical based on a fictionalized account of the life of Margaret Brown, who survived the sinking of the *Titanic*. A movie of the same title was released in 1964.

1985   Robert Ballard, leading a joint American-French expedition, discovers the remains of the *Titanic*.

1986 Ballard returns to the wreckage site, descends in a submersible, and views the *Titanic* in person.

Congress passes the Titanic Maritime Memorial Act to encourage international efforts to designate the shipwreck of the *Titanic* as an international maritime memorial and to provide for reasonable research, exploration, and salvage of the shipwreck.

1987 Another French-American expedition visits the *Titanic* and removes artifacts. Ballard opposes taking items from the wreckage.

1994 A maritime court in Virginia upholds the claims of RMS Titanic, Inc., to become "salvor-in-possession" of the ship on June 7.

An exhibit of items salvaged from the *Titanic* opens in London on October 4.

1997 James Cameron's blockbuster movie, *Titanic*, is released on December 18.

1998 RMS Titanic, Inc., succeeds in bringing a section of the *Titanic*'s hull, weighing 17 to 18 tons (15 to 16 metric tons) to the United States.

2003 *Ghosts of the Abyss*, a documentary by James Cameron, opens.

2004 Robert Ballard makes a return visit to the *Titanic*.

2005 Ocean explorers and television hosts Richie Kohler and John Chatterton find huge sections of the bottom of the *Titanic* on the ocean floor. Their discovery raises new speculations about the way the ship sank.

2009 Millvina Dean, the last *Titanic* survivor, dies on May 31 at the age of ninety-seven.

2010 RMS Titanic, Inc., launches an expedition to create three-dimensional maps of the wreckage area.

2012 A memorial cruise is scheduled to commemorate the one-hundredth anniversary of the sinking of the *Titanic*.

GLOSSARY OF NAUTICAL TERMS

boatswain: a supervisor of unlicensed deckhands

bow: the front portion of a ship

bridge: the navigation area of a ship from which the captain charts the course and from which communications are made

bulkhead: a sturdy dividing wall separating areas of a ship

crow's nest: a high platform from which the lookout scans the horizon

davit: a specialized pulley for lowering lifeboats into the ocean

funnel: a ship's smokestack

gantry: framework, or scaffolding, used in building a ship

growler: an iceberg less than 50 feet (15 m) long and 15 feet (4.5 m) high

hull: the main body of a ship

ice field: a large area of ice, often several miles wide

keel: the central lowermost plank that stretches from bow to stern forming the central structural element of a ship

knot: a measure of nautical speed; about 1.2 miles (1.9 km) per hour

maritime: having to do with the sea

master-at-arms: a ship official in charge of security and law enforcement

Morse lamp: a blinker lamp for signaling in Morse code

port: the left-hand side of a ship

rusticle: an underwater rust formation that occurs when oxygen interacts with wrought iron. A variety of bacteria and fungi feed on the rust, releasing products that become part of the rusticle.

starboard: the right-hand side of a ship

steerage: the least expensive accommodations on a passenger ship; also known as third class

stern: the rear portion of a ship

stoker: a crew member who tends a ship's furnace

submersible: a small manned exploration vessel, which descends from a surface ship deep into the ocean

well deck: an enclosed area toward the stern of a ship that is sandwiched between a higher deck area on one side and rooms rising from the deck on the other

wireless: telegraph machine capable of transmitting on radio waves rather than over wires

WHAT HAPPENED TO THEM?

The Fates of Ships
Associated with the Titanic

Britannic: The third ship envisioned by Bruce Ismay and Lord Pirrie, the *Gigantic*, was renamed the *Britannic* after the *Titanic* sank. The White Star Line no longer wished to emphasize the immensity of their ships since the huge size of the *Titanic* hadn't saved it from disaster. Launched in 1914, the *Britannic* became a hospital ship in World War I. After hitting a mine or being struck by a German torpedo during World War I in 1916, it sank.

Californian: The *Californian*, which arrived on the scene after the *Titanic* had sunk, was torpedoed by a German submarine in November 1915 during World War I and sank.

Carpathia: The *Carpathia* was used to transport U.S. troops to Europe during World War I. En route from Liverpool, England, to Boston, Massachusetts, the ship was torpedoed by a German submarine and sank on July 17, 1918. A total of 275 of the 289 people aboard were saved.

Lusitania: The widely heralded British ship, with which the *Titanic* was designed to compete, was torpedoed by a German U-Boat on May 7, 1915. Nearly 1,200 people died, including 114 Americans. The incident caused a public furor and helped turn the tide of opinion in the United States against Germany. In 1917 the United States joined World War I by declaring war on Germany.

Olympic: After the *Titanic* sank, the *Olympic* was refitted with more lifeboats. Her bulkheads were raised to prevent flooding, and her hull received a new inner skin. After serving as a naval transport ship during World War I, the ship resumed its runs for the White Star Line. By the time the vessel was retired in 1935, it had crossed the Atlantic Ocean hundreds of times. The ship was stripped of most of its fittings, which were auctioned off and moved to various British public buildings and homes. Some of the original wood panels were purchased by Celebrity Cruises of the United States and appear in an onboard restaurant on its cruise ship *Millennium*.

SOURCE NOTES

7 Robert D. Ballard and Michael S. Sweeney, *Return to the* Titanic: *A New Look at the World's Most Famous Lost Ship* (Washington, DC: National Geographic, 2004), 28.

7 Don Lynch, Titanic: *An Illustrated History* (1992; repr., Edison, NJ: Wellfleet Press, 2006), 85.

7 Ibid.

7 Ibid.

7 Ballard and Sweeney, 28–29.

7 Ibid., 29.

7 Lynch, 89.

8 Ibid., 91.

8 Ibid.

9 Susan Wels, Titanic: *Legacy of the World's Greatest Ocean Liner* (San Diego: Time-Life Books, 1997), 86.

9 Walter Lord, *A Night to Remember* (New York: Henry Holt and Company, 1983), 37.

9 Wels, 12.

9 Ibid.

10–11 "*Titanic*—Jack Thayer's Own Story of the Wreck," Logoi.com, n.d., http://www.logoi.com/notes/titanic/jack_thayers_story_wreck.html (July 20, 2010).

11 Lynch, 139.

12 Speedwell Village, "The S.S. *Savannah*," 1981, n.d., http:www.morrisparks.net/speedwell/sss/sss.html (December 13, 2010).

13 Wels, 12.

13 "S.S. Oceanic," *Titanic* and Other White Star Ships, n.d., http://www.titanic-whitestarships.com/Oceanic1_1871.htm (November 4, 2010).

16 Nick Barratt, *Lost Voices from the* Titanic: *The Definitive Oral History* (New York: Palgrave Macmillan, 2010), 19.

16 Ibid.

16 Wels, 26.

16 Barratt, 37.

19 Ibid., 59.

21 Ibid., 75.

21 Ibid.

23 Wels, 61.

23 Barratt, 80.

23 Stephanie Barczewski, Titanic: *A Night Remembered* (London: Hambledon & London, 2004), 5.

23 Ibid., 9.

24 Father Browne's Home Page, "Frank Browne, Photographer of the *Titanic*," Titanic Photographs.com, n.d., http://www.fatherbrowne.com/BiographyText.htm (September 4, 2010).

24 Ibid.

25 Barratt, 73.

25 Charles Herbert Lightoller, Titanic *and Other Ships* (London: Ivor Nicholson & Watson, 1935), 5.

25 Barratt, 86.

26 Wels, 80.

26 Ibid.

26–27 Ibid., 83.

27 Barczewski, 13–14.

27 Beau Riffenburgh, *The* Titanic *Experience* (London: Carlton Publishing, 2008), 27.

27 Barczewski, 14.

28 Lightoller, 174.

28 Ibid.

28 Ibid.

29 Barczewski, 18.

29 Barratt, 125.

30 Ibid., 133.

30 Ibid.

30 Lord, 10.

30 Barczewski, 19.

30–31 Lynch, 97.

31–32 Wels, 88.

32 Ibid.

32 Lynch, 109.

33 Wels, 96.

33 Ibid.

33 Ibid.

33 Lynch, 115.

34 Ibid., 108.

35 Ibid., 110.

35 Lord, 112.

35 Ibid.

35 Lord, 51.

36 Lynch, 110.

37 Encyclopedia Titanica, "Guggenheim, Dying, Sent Wife Message," *New York Times*, April 20, 1912, 2010, http://www.encyclopedia-titanica.org/guggenheim-dying-sent-wife-message.html (July 15, 2010).

39 Lynch, 133.

39 Ibid., 135.

40 Barczewski, 27.

40 Lightoller, 188.

40 Lord, 84.

40 Lightoller, 191.

41 Lord, 97.

41 Ibid., 98.

41 Ibid.

42 Lynch, 144.

43 Lynch, 148.

43 Lord, 108.

43 Ibid.

43 Ibid.

44 Lord, 110–111.

45 John R. Henderson, *Demographics of the* TITANIC *Passengers: Deaths, Survivals, and Lifeboat Occupancy*, Ithaca College Library, January 20, 2011, http://www.ithaca.edu/staff/jhenderson/titanic.html#crew (January 23, 2011)

47 Lord, 123.

48 Barczewski, 33.

48 Lord, 125.

49 Encyclopedia Titanica, "Captain Rostron, *Titanic* Rescuer: Raced through Icy Waters to Save 700 Persons— Dies in England at 71," *New York Times*, November 6, 1940, 2010, http://www.encyclopedia-titanica.org/captain-rostron-titanic-rescuer.html (August 15, 2010).

49 Ibid.

50 Lynch, 150.

50 Ibid.

50 Ibid.

50 Lord, 130.

52 Ibid.

53 Judith B. Geller, Titanic: *Women and Children First* (New York: W. W. Norton, 1998), 164.

53 Ibid., 163.

55 Barczewski, 47.

55 Riffenburgh, 44.

55 Brad Matsen, Titanic's *Last Secrets: The Further Adventures of Shadow Divers John Chatterton and Richie Kohler* (New York: Twelve, 2008), 178.

55 Barczewski, 48.

55 Ohio University, "Carr V. Van Anda Biography," E. W. Scripps School of Journalism, n.d., http://scrippsjschool .org/about/carrvananda.php (August 21, 2010).

55 Barczewski, 49.

57 Harold Bride, "Thrilling Story by *Titanic*'s Surviving Wireless Man," *New York Times*, April 19, 1912, http://query.nytimes. com/mem/archivefree/pdf?r es = F10D11FE3E5813738DD DA00994DC405B828DF1D3 (January 20, 2011).

59 Matsen, 197.

60 Walter Lord, *The Night Lives On* (New York: Avon Books, 1986), 163.

61 Barczewski, 79.

61 Lightoller, 195.

61 Barczewski, 68.

61 Ibid., 69.

61 Ibid., 67.

61 W. B. Bartlett, Titanic: *9 Hours to Hell, the Survivors' Story* (London: Amberly Publishing, 2010), 298.

61 Ibid.

62 Matsen, 191.

62 Barratt, 214.

62 Ibid., 218.

63 Barczewski, 70.

63 Ibid.

63 *Literary Digest*, "The Two *"Titanic"* Investigations," n.d., http://www .oldmagazinearticles .com/pdf/TITANIC-Report .PDF (July 10, 2010).

64 Richard Allene, "*Titanic* Sunk by Steering Blunder,

New Book Claims," *London Telegraph*, September 21, 2010, http://www.telegraph .co.uk/culture/books/ booknews/8016752/Titanic- sunk-by-steering-blunder-new- book-claims.html (September 30, 2010).

64 Ibid.

65 Senan Molony, Titanic *and the Mystery Ship* (Gloucestershire, UK: Tempus Publishing, 2006), 326.

66 Bartlett, 129.

66 Ibid., 130.

66 Ibid.

66 Ibid., 305.

69 Geller, 106.

69 Ibid., 105.

69 Ibid., 37.

69 Encyclopedia Titanica, "Mrs. Margaret Brown (nee Tobin)," n.d., Encyclopedia Titanica, http://www.encyclopedia- titanica.org/titanic-biography/ molly-brown.html (August 5, 2010).

71 Yahoo, "Hero of SS *Titanic* Archibald Gracie IV, Bronx, NY," flickr, 2010, http://www

.flickr.com/photos/23021987@N06/2483708253 (September 3, 2010).

72   Encyclopedia Titanica, "Miss Violet Constance Jessop," Encyclopedia Titanica, 2010, http://www.encyclopedia-titanica.org/titanic-biography/violet-constance-jessop.html (September 3, 2010).

74   Encyclopedia Titanica, "Miss Dorothy Winifred Gibson," Encyclopedia Titanica, 2010, http://www.encyclopedia-titanica.org/titanic-biography/dorothy-gibson.html (October 1, 2010).

74   Titanic Historical Society, "A Tribute to Winnifred (Quick) Van Tongerloo: Recalling One of the Last Titanic Survivors," titanic1.org, 2010, http://www.titanic1.org/people/winnifred-van-tongerloo3.asp (September 3, 2010).

75   Chicago Tribune, "Mary Rourke, Titanic's Last Survivor: Millvina Dean, 97," Swamp, n.d., http://www.swamppolitics.com/news/politics/blog/2009/05/titanics_last_survivor_milvina.html (September 3, 2010).

75   John F. Burns, "Millvina Dean, Titanic's Last Survivor, Dies at 97," New York Times, June 1, 2009, http://www.nytimes/2009/06/01/world/europe/01dean.html (September 3, 2010).

75   BBC, "Last Titanic Survivor Dies at 97," BBC News, March 2, 2010, http://news.bbc.co.uk/2/hi/uk_news/england/hampshire/8070095.stm (September 3, 2010).

75   Chicago Tribune.

78   American Academy of Achievement, "Robert Ballard Interview—Academy of Achievement," February 13, 1991, Academy of Achievement, 2010, http://www.achievement.org/autodoc/bal0int-1 (August 1, 2010).

79   Ballard and Sweeney, 39.

80   Ibid.

80   Robert D. Ballard and Malcolm McConnell, Adventures in Ocean Exploration: From the Discovery of the Titanic to the Search for Noah's Flood (Washington, DC: National Geographic, 2001), 136.

81   Ibid., 137.

81   Ibid.

81   CBS News, "Bob Ballard, the Great Explorer: Lara Logan Profiles the Ocean Explorer, Who Not Only Found the Titanic, but Also Made Scientific Discoveries," 60 Minutes, November 29, 2009, http://www.cbsnews.com/stories/2009/11/25/60minutes/main5773673.shtml (July 10, 2010).

81   Ballard and Sweeney, 42.

81   American Academy of Achievement.

82   Robert D. Ballard and Rick Archbold, The Discovery of the Titanic (New York: Warner / Madison Press Book, 1987), 90.

82   Ibid., 91.

82   Ballard and Sweeney, 53.

83   Ibid.

83   Ibid.

83   American Academy of Achievement.

83   Ballard and Sweeney, 57.

83   American Academy of Achievement.

84   Ibid.

84   Ibid.

84   Ibid.

84   Ibid.

84   Ibid.

84   Ibid.

84   Will Sellers, "A *Titanic* Tale: A Former Alvin Pilot Recalls His 1986 Dives on the Shipwreck," *Oceanus*, September 2, 2010, http://www.whoi.edu/oceanus/viewarticle.do?archives = trve&id = 80686 (September 30, 2010).

85   CBS News.

85   Ibid.

85   American Academy of Achievement.

86   Ricardo J. Elia, "Diving for Diamonds," *Archaeology*, September 20, 2000, http://www.archaeology.org/online/features/titanic/index.html (September 8, 2010).

88   Ballard and Sweeney, 73–74.

88   William F. Buckley Jr., "Down to the Great Ship," *New York Times*, October 18, 1987, http://www.nytimes.com/1987/10/18/magazine/down-to-the-great-ship.html (July 18, 2010).

89   Ballard and Sweeney, 166.

90–91   William Tuohy, "82 Years after Sinking, *Titanic* Still in Spotlight," August 13, 1994, available online at the Library of Virginia, n.d., http://www.lva.virginia.gov/exhibs/titanic/new/spot.htm (September 3, 2010).

92   Wels, 148.

93   Robert Ballard, "Interview: Robert Ballard Discusses the Current State of the Wreckage of the *Titanic*," interview by Steve Inskeep, *Morning Edition*, NPR, June 3, 2004, available online at http://www.highbeam.com/doc/1P1-95177473.html (January 20 2011).

94–95   James Cameron, "James Cameron: *Playboy* Interview," interviewed by *Playboy Magazine*, December 2009, http://www.playboy.com/articles/james-cameron-interview/index.html?page = 2 (September 3, 2010).

95   Don Lynch and Ken Marschall, *Ghosts of the Abyss: A Journey into the Heart of the* Titanic (Toronto: Da Capo Press, 2003), 11.

96   "The Art of Ken Marschall," n.d., http://www.kenmarschall.com (September 3, 2010).

97   Matsen, 226.

SELECTED BIBLIOGRAPHY

Ballard, Robert D., and Malcolm McConnell. *Adventures in Ocean Exploration: From the Discovery of the* Titanic *to the Search for Noah's Flood.* Washington, DC: National Geographic, 2001.

Ballard, Robert D., and Rick Archbold. *The Discovery of the* Titanic. New York: Warner / Madison Press Book, 1987.

———. *Lost Liners.* New York: Hyperion, 1997.

Ballard, Robert D., and Michael S. Sweeney. *Return to the* Titanic: *A New Look at the World's Most Famous Lost Ship.* Washington, DC: National Geographic, 2004.

Barczewski, Stephanie. Titanic: *A Night Remembered.* London: Hambledon & London, 2004.

Barratt, Nick. *Lost Voices from the* Titanic: *The Definitive Oral History.* New York: Palgrave Macmillan, 2010.

Bartlett, W. B. Titanic: *9 Hours to Hell, the Survivors' Story.* London: Amberly Publishing, 2010.

CBS News. "Bob Ballard, the Great Explorer: Lara Logan Profiles the Ocean Explorer, Who Not Only Found the *Titanic,* but Also Made Scientific Discoveries." *60 Minutes.* November 29, 2009. http://www. cbsnews.com/stories/2009/11/25/60minutes/ main5773673.shtml (July 10, 2010).

Geller, Judith B. Titanic: *Women and Children First.* New York: W. W. Norton, 1998.

Goubeaux, Rob, and Violet Jessop. Titanic's *Final Moments: Missing Pieces.* DVD. New York: A & E Television Networks, 1996.

Lightoller, Charles Herbert. Titanic *and Other Ships.* London: Ivor Nicholson & Watson, 1935.

Lord, Walter. *The Night Lives On.* New York: Avon Books, 1986.

———. *A Night to Remember.* New York: Henry Holt and Company, 1983.

Lynch, Don. Titanic: *An Illustrated History.* 1992. Reprint, Edison, NJ: Wellfleet Press, 2006.

Lynch, Don, and Ken Marschall. *Ghosts of the Abyss: A Journey into the Heart of the* Titanic. Toronto: Da Capo Press, 2003.

Matsen, Brad. Titanic's *Last Secrets: The Further Adventures of Shadow Divers John Chatterton and Richie Kohler.* New York: Twelve, 2008.

McCarty, Jennifer Hooper, and Tim Foecke. *What Really Sank the* Titanic: *New Forensic Discoveries.* New York: Citadel Press, 2008.

Molony, Senan. Titanic *and the Mystery Ship.* Gloucestershire, UK: Tempus Publishing, 2006.

O'Donnell, E. E. Foreword by Dr. Robert D. Ballard. *The Last Days of the* Titanic: *Photographs and Mementos of the Tragic Maiden Voyage.* Niwot, CO: Roberts Rinehart Publishers. First published 1997 by Wolfhound Press, Dublin.

Paxton, Bill, Don Lynch, Ken Marschall, and Charles Pellegrino. *Ghosts of the Abyss.* DVD. Burbank, CA: Walt Disney Video, 2004.

Peltier, Melissa Jo. Titanic: *The Complete Story.* DVD. New York: A & E Television Networks, 1994.

Riffenburgh, Beau. *The* Titanic *Experience.* London: Carlton Publishing, 2008.

Streissguth, Thomas, ed. *The Sinking of the* Titanic. San Diego: Greenhaven, 2001.

Thresh, Peter. Titanic: *The Truth behind the Disaster.* Hills, MN: Crescent Publishing, 1992.

Wade, Wyn Craig. *The* Titanic: *End of a Dream.* New York: Penguin Books, 1992.

Wels, Susan. Titanic: *Legacy of the World's Greatest Ocean Liner.* San Diego: Time-Life Books, 1997.

Winocour. Jack. *The Story of the* Titanic *as Told by Its Survivors, Lawrence Beesley, Archibald Gracie, Commander Lightoller, Harold Bride.* Mineola, NY: Dover Publications, 1960.

FURTHER INFORMATION

BOOKS

Adams, Sam. *Eyewitness* Titanic. London: DK Publishing, 1999.

Ballard, Robert D. *Exploring the* Titanic: *How the Greatest Ship Ever Lost Was Found.* Reprint, 1988; Toronto: Black Walnut / Madison Press, 2010.

Bortz, Fred. *Seven Wonders of Exploration Technology.* Minneapolis: Twenty-First Century Books, 2010.

Brewster, Hugh. *882½ Amazing Answers to Your Questions about the* Titanic. New York: Scholastic, 1999.

Brewster, Ken. *Inside the* Titanic. New York: Little, Brown, and Company, 1997.

Brown, Don. *All Stations! Distress: April 15, 1912: The Day the* Titanic *Sank.* New York: Roaring Brook Press, 2008.

Hill, Christine M. *Robert Ballard: Oceanographer Who Discovered the* Titanic. Berkeley Heights, NJ: Enslow, 1999.

Tanaka, Shelley. *On Board the* Titanic: *What It Was Like When the Great Liner Sank.* Toronto: Black Walnut / Madison Press, 2010.

Tarshis, Lauren. *I Survived the Sinking of the* Titanic. New York: Scholastic, 2010.

White, Ellen Emerson. *Voyage on the Great* Titanic; *The Diary of Margaret Ann Brady.* Dear America series. New York: Scholastic, 2010.

Williams, Barbara. Titanic *Crossing.* New York: Scholastic, 1997.

Yount, Lisa. *Robert Ballard: Explorer and Undersea Archaeologist.* New York: Chelsea House, 2009.

WEBSITES

Encyclopedia Titanica
http://www.encyclopedia-titanica.org/
This comprehensive site includes links to basic facts, a timeline, passenger and crew lists, survivor biographies, and more.

"I Survived the *Titanic*"
http://www.nationalgeographic.com/media/world/9607/titanic/html
This excerpt from *World Magazine* relates the true experiences of twelve-year-old Ruth Becker on the *Titanic* and in a lifeboat.

Robert Ballard Biography—Academy of Achievement
http://www.achievement.org/autodoc/page/
bal0bio-1
This site spotlights the man who discovered the *Titanic* and includes links to an interview and photo gallery.

RMS Titanic, Inc.
http://www.rmstitanic.net/
This is the official website of the only organization with the legal right to salvage items from the *Titanic* wreck. It includes (among other items) links to artifacts, exhibitions, conservation, science, and frequently asked questions.

Titanic
http://www.kidskonnect.com/subject-index/16-histoory/281-titanic.html
Aimed at young people, this site includes fast facts, statistics, and a variety of links to more information about the *Titanic*.

Titanic Facts
http://www.titanic-facts.com/
This site includes links to the history of the ship, the passengers, photos, the movie, and more.

The Titanic Historical Society
http://www.titanic1.org/
The official website of the Titanic Historical Society based in Massachusetts allows you to access articles, events, and the museum store.

The *Titanic* Photographs
http://www.titanicphotographs.com/
The story of *Titanic* passenger Father Browne is told on this site. Links are also provided to his photographs, the last photos taken of the *Titanic*.

DVDs

Ghosts of the Abyss. Directed by James Cameron. Los Angeles: Walt Disney Video, 2004.

A Night to Remember. Directed by Roy Ward Baker. New York: Criterion, 1998.

Secrets of the Titanic. Directed by Robert D. Ballard and Nicolas Noxon. Washington DC: National Geographic Video, 1999.

Titanic. Directed by James Cameron. Hollywood, CA: Paramount, 1997.

The Unsinkable Molly Brown. Directed by Charles Walters. Burbank, CA: Warner Home Video, 2000.

LERNER
SOURCE
Expand learning beyond the printed book. Download free, complementary educational resources for this book from our website, www.lerneresource.com.

INDEX

ABOUT THE AUTHOR

Stephanie Sammartino McPherson wrote her first children's story in college. She enjoyed the process so much that she's never stopped writing. A former teacher and freelance newspaper writer, she has written twenty-eight books and numerous magazine stories. Her most recent book is a biography of Sergey Brin and Larry Page, the founders of Google. She and her husband, Richard, live in Virginia but also call California home. They are the parents of two grown children.

PHOTO ACKNOWLEDGMENTS

The images in this book are used with the permission of: © Central Press/Getty Images, pp. 2, 12; © Max Dannenbaum/Stone/Getty Images, p. 5; Painting by Ken Marschall © 1992, p. 6; © Mary Evans/Onslow Auctions/The Image Works, p. 7; The Granger Collection, New York, pp. 8, 21, 49; © Bettmann/CORBIS, pp. 11, 38, 43, 46, 60; Lord Pirrie and J Bruce Ismay inspecting hull (HOYFM.HW.H23640), © National Museums Northern Ireland, Collection Harland & Wolff, Ulster Folk & Transport Museum, p. 14; Library of Congress, pp. 15 (top, LC-USZ62-76281), 18 (LC-USZ62-34781), 20 (left, LC-USZ62-116096), 20 (right, LC-USZ62-26812), 23 (LC-USZ62-116052), 30 (LC-DIG-ggbain-19397), 51 (left, LC-USZ62-116090), 51 (top right, LC-USZ62-99341), 51 (bottom right, LC-USZ62-56453), 59 (LC-USZ62-59074), 62 (LC-USZ62-68081), 70 (LC-USZ62-94037), 73 (LC-DIG-hec-00939), 74 (LC-G412-T-4996-002); ITV/Rex Features USA, p. 15 (bottom); © F.J. Mortimer/Hulton Archive/Getty Images, p. 17; © TopFoto/The Image Works, pp. 19, 64; © Trinity Mirror/Mirrorpix/Alamy, p. 22; © akg-images/Universal Images Group, pp. 24 (both), 34; © Mary Evans/National Archives/The Image Works, p. 26; AP Photo/Matthew Cavanaugh, p. 27; The Art Archive/Ocean Memorabilia Collection, p. 28; © New York Public Library/Photo Researchers, Inc., p. 29; © Mary Evans Picture Library/The Image Works, p. 31; The Mariners' Museum, Newport News, VA, p. 35; © Laura Westlund/Independent Picture Service, pp. 37, 48; National Archives, p. 39; © The Stapleton Collection/The Bridgeman Art Library, p. 40; © National Maritime Museum, Greenwich, UK, p. 41; © Leon Neal/AFP/Getty Images, p. 42; © Hulton Archive/Getty Images, p. 47; © Underwood & Underwood/CORBIS, pp. 54, 56; © Mansell/Time & Life Pictures/Getty Images, p. 57; © Whitlock/Hulton Archive/Getty Images, p. 63; © Monica Wells PCL/SuperStock, p. 67; © akg-images/Universal Images Group/The Image Works, p. 68; © Gerry Penny/AFP/Getty Images, p. 75; © Ralph White/CORBIS, pp. 76, 79, 80, 81, 83, 86, 87, 88; © Hank Morgan/Photo Researchers, Inc., p. 78; AP Photo/NOAA, p. 89; © Matthew Polak/Sygma/CORBIS, p. 90; © David Paul Morris/Getty Images, p. 91; 20th Century Fox/Paramount/Wallace, Merie W./The Kobal Collection, p. 94; Painting by Ken Marschall © 1996, p. 96.

Front cover: © Max Dannenbaum/Stone/Getty Images. Back cover: AP Photo.

Main body text set in ITC Slimbach Std Book 11/16
Typeface provided by International Typeface Corp.